MW00959322

COLORADO TRAVEL GUIDE 2023

Unveiling the iconic landmark and natural splendors: Itinerary, hidden gems, sightseeing, essentials,for first timer

Wesley J.Ray

Table of Contents

Preface

Welcome to Colorado, a beautiful state with gorgeous scenery, thrilling experiences, and a thriving culture. With a wealth of knowledge, expert advice, and inspiration, this handbook is meant to be your travel companion as you set out on a tour around the Centennial State. It will help you make the most of your time in Colorado.

You will find a thorough examination of Colorado's geographical characteristics, climate, travel needs, modes of transportation, lodging alternatives, and important packing advice within these pages. The marvels of well-known sites like Rocky Mountain National Park, Mesa Verde, Garden of the Gods, and the lovely Maroon Bells will come to light for you. Enjoy the state's numerous eating and nightlife options, engage in outdoor activities and leisure, and immerse yourself in its cultural and aesthetic treasures.

We will lead you through the must-see sights, hidden jewels, and immersive experiences that are waiting for you, from the busy streets of Denver to the quaint villages of Aspen, Boulder, and Colorado Springs. Colorado provides a wide range of options to satisfy your travel needs, whether you're looking for exhilarating outdoor activities, cultural encounters in bustling cities, or a tranquil retreat in hot springs and spa resorts.

As you explore Colorado's beauties, this handbook seeks to enlighten you with information, provide helpful guidance, and pique your interest and sense of awe. We hope that this book will be your go-to travel companion, whether you are a frequent traveler or a first-time visitor, assisting you in making priceless memories and forging a close connection with Colorado's extraordinary beauty and spirit.

Prepare yourself to set out on an exciting tour, take in the clean mountain air, see breathtaking scenery, and get engrossed in the rich tapestry of Colorado's culture and natural beauty. Allow this book to serve as your entranceway to the delights Colorado has to offer. Travel safely!

Introduction

Summary of Colorado

Colorado, a fascinating state in the west of the country, is renowned for its breathtaking natural beauty, varied landscapes, and outdoor leisure options. Wyoming, Nebraska, Kansas, Oklahoma, New Mexico, Utah, and Arizona form its northern, northeastern, eastern, eastern, and southeast borders, respectively. Colorado is sometimes referred to as the "Centennial State" since it became a state in 1876, precisely 100 years after the United States Declaration of Independence was signed.

The spectacular Rocky Mountains, which dominate Colorado's western half, are what define the state's topography. Mesas, undulating hills, and high plains make up the eastern region. The "Fourteeners"—peaks in Colorado that are higher than 14,000 feet—include well-known summits like Pikes Peak and Longs Peak. Outdoor enthusiasts from all over the globe go to these mountains to walk, climb, ski, and take in the spectacular alpine beauty.

Colorado is home to a wide variety of natural beauties in addition to its mountains. It is the location of magnificent national parks including the Great Sand Dunes National Park and Preserve, Rocky Mountain National Park, and Mesa Verde National Park. Incomparable options for hiking, animal watching, camping, and discovering old archaeological sites are provided by these parks.

The climate in Colorado varies greatly from area to region. Because of the lower temperatures and more snowfall brought on by the mountains' high altitudes, it is a well-liked vacation spot for those who like winter sports. While the southwest of Colorado has a climate more akin to a desert, the eastern plains have a drier, more moderate temperature.

Denver, the biggest city in the state and its capitol, is located in the Front Range Urban Corridor. Denver is a dynamic, multicultural city well-known for its major sports teams, rich culinary choices, and burgeoning arts and culture scene. Other significant cities in Colorado include Colorado Springs, which is the location of the well-known Garden of the Gods, Boulder, which is recognized for its outdoor recreation options and college town vibe, and Aspen, which is a premier ski resort and a major cultural center.

Colorado's smaller towns and villages provide genuine experiences and emanate a certain appeal away from the city. There are a lot of undiscovered treasures in the state, whether you want to explore old mining towns like

Breckenridge and Telluride or learn about Greeley's agricultural past.

Overall, Colorado's beauty may be attributed to its beautiful natural scenery, recreational activities, historical history, and kind people. It is a place that appeals to those who like the outdoors, history, and a bustling metropolitan atmosphere. Colorado guarantees a distinctive and unique experience for every tourist, whether they are hiking through alpine meadows, skiing down snowy slopes, or immersing themselves in the cultural treasures of its towns and cities.

Geographic Characteristics

Colorado is fortunate to have a wide variety of geographical characteristics, which add to its breathtaking scenery. Here are some of the state's distinctive geographical characteristics, which range from imposing mountains to wide plains:

Rocky Mountains: The gorgeous Rocky Mountains, which span the state from north to south, are mostly located in Colorado. The stunning summits of this renowned mountain range include the renowned Fourteeners, or peaks higher than 14,000 feet in height, including Pikes Peak, Mount Evans, Longs Peak, and many more. The Rocky Mountains are home to a wealth of species, clear lakes, flowing waterfalls, and breathtaking alpine vistas.

Great Plains: The immense plains that traverse the eastern part of Colorado are its defining feature. Rolling hills, meadows, and agricultural regions may be found in these high plains, often referred to as the Colorado Piedmont. The plains are a significant component of Colorado's agriculture sector and provide a stark contrast to the rough mountain scenery.

Colorado Plateau: In the state's southwest, Colorado shares a section of the Colorado Plateau, a vast area distinguished by its distinctive geology and eye-catching red rock formations. This region is home to well-known attractions like Mesa Verde National Park, whose ancient cliff dwellings reveal the region's Native American past, and the breathtaking Colorado River gorges, including the well-known Black Canyon of the Gunnison National Park.

High Desert: Arid conditions and few vegetation are characteristics of the high desert habitat found in parts of western and southern Colorado. Mesas, buttes, and sand dunes are just a few of the unusual terrain features found in this area. A prominent example of

Colorado's high desert splendor is the Great Sand Dunes National Park and Preserve, which has towering dunes set against the background of the Sangre de Cristo Mountains.

Colorado River: One of the state's main streams is the Colorado River. Its source is in the Rocky Mountains, and as it passes into Colorado, it sculpts steep gorges and supplies water for agriculture and hydroelectric power. The river is well known for its outdoor activities, which include rafting, fishing, and picturesque boat rides.

Lakes and Reservoirs: Colorado is home to a large number of both natural and man-made lakes and reservoirs. One of them is the renowned Lake Dillon, which is close to Breckenridge and provides spectacular views of the nearby mountains. Grand Lake, the biggest natural lake in the state, and Blue Mesa Reservoir, the biggest body of water in

Colorado, are two further noteworthy bodies of water.

Natural hot springs with geothermally heated mineral water provide a soothing and healing experience may be found all across Colorado. There are hot springs spread out around the state, including notable spots like Glenwood Springs, Ouray, and Pagosa Springs.

These geographical characteristics help to create Colorado's varied and alluring landscapes, drawing tourists from all over the globe looking for outdoor activities, visual splendor, and chances to get close to nature.

Weather and climate

Colorado's different heights and geographic characteristics result in a wide variety of climates. The majority of the state's climate is classified as a semiarid continental climate with clear seasonal fluctuations. The climate and weather of Colorado may be summarized as follows:

High Elevation: Colorado has the greatest average elevation of any state in the union, which has a big impact on its climate. Increased elevation typically results in colder temperatures and thinner air, which lowers atmospheric pressure and lowers humidity.

Colorado has four different seasons: spring, summer, autumn, and winter, each with its own distinct weather patterns and leisure activities. Seasonal changeovers may happen quickly, particularly at higher altitudes.

Colorado has significant regional and altitude-related temperature variations. Summers are often warm and pleasant, with lowland average temperatures between the 70s to 90s Fahrenheit (20s to 30s Celsius). Higher altitudes have colder average temperatures, and even in the summer, the evenings may be chilly. In the lowlands, winter temperatures often range from the 20s to the 40s Fahrenheit (-6 to 4 degrees Celsius). Even lower temperatures are prevalent in mountainous places, with high summits often seeing sub-zero temperatures.

Colorado is well-known for its copious amounts of sunlight and bright sky. With over 300 days of sunlight on average each year, the state is a great place to enjoy outdoor activities and winter sports. However, because of the increased UV radiation caused by high elevation and a thinner atmosphere, sunscreen and protective gear are crucial.

Precipitation: The geography and season have an impact on Colorado's precipitation patterns. Less precipitation falls in the eastern plains and high deserts, which average 12 to 20 inches (30 to 50 cm) yearly. Orographic lift—when moist air is propelled upward by the mountains—causes the mountainous areas to receive more precipitation, particularly the western slope of the Rockies. In the mountains during the winter, snowfall is frequent and creates ideal skiing and snowboarding conditions.

Thunderstorms: Throughout the summer, Colorado is renowned for its frequent afternoon thunderstorms. These storms may be severe and include lightning, high gusts, and copious amounts of rain. Hail and, sometimes, flash floods may also result from thunderstorms in the highlands.

Microclimates: The various geography and altitudes of Colorado provide microclimates, where the weather may change greatly over relatively small distances. For instance, compared to the high alpine regions, the Front Range, which includes towns like Denver and Boulder, has milder winters and warmer summers.

Remember that Colorado's weather may change quickly, particularly in mountainous areas, so it's best to check the local predictions and be ready for abrupt changes in temperature and weather.

Preparing for your Trip

Travel requirements and documentation

Understanding the travel papers and procedures needed for admission into the United States and the state of Colorado is vital while organizing a trip to Colorado. The important factors are as follows:

Passport: If you're coming from another nation to Colorado, you'll need a current passport. Make sure your passport is valid for at least six months after the day you want to travel.

Visa Waiver Program: Under the Visa Waiver Program (VWP), nationals of several nations may be permitted to visit the United States. Through this program, qualified visitors may enter the country for up to 90 days without a visa for leisure or business. However, before boarding an aircraft to the United States, prior authorisation through the Electronic System for Travel authorisation (ESTA) is necessary. Verify your nation's participation in the VWP and, if necessary, submit an ESTA application.

Visa: Prior to going to Colorado, if you are not qualified for the Visa Waiver Program, you must get a U.S. visa. The kind of visa you need depends depend on whether you're traveling for business, pleasure, or education. For information on individual visa requirements and application processes, get in touch with the American embassy or consulate in your country of residence.

Entry Requirements for COVID-19: Due to the continuing COVID-19 pandemic, there may be particular entry standards and travel limitations in effect. Check the most recent Centers for Disease Control and Prevention (CDC) recommendations as well as any travel warnings issued by the governments of your home country and the United States. These prerequisites can include immunization documentation, a negative COVID-19 test result, or an initial quarantine period.

Customs Declaration: You must fill out a customs declaration form with information about the goods you are carrying into the United States when you get there. Be prepared to declare any products or commodities that might be subject to limitations or taxes from customs.

A valid driver's license from your home country or an international driving permit (IDP) are required if you want to drive in Colorado. It is important to always have your passport and a form of photo identification on you for identification.

Travel insurance that covers medical costs, trip cancellation or interruption, and other unexpected occurrences is strongly advised, even if it is not a legal necessity. Make sure your insurance policy offers sufficient protection for your trip to Colorado by reviewing it.

Travel regulations might change over time, so it's important to remain up to date. Consult the U.S. before leaving. Department of State, the U.S. For the most recent information on travel documentation and regulations, see the Customs and Border Protection website and the applicable embassy or consulate.

Options for Transportation

In order to aid visitors in navigating the state and discovering its many attractions, Colorado provides a variety of transportation choices. Here are a some of the various modes of transportation:

Air travel: Colorado is serviced by a number of significant airports, including one of the busiest airports in the country, Denver International Airport

(DEN). Denver International Airport serves as a convenient entry point to Colorado with its many domestic and international airline options. Additionally, smaller regional airports like Aspen/Pitkin County Airport (ASE) and Colorado Springs Airport (COS) provide connectivity to certain state areas.

Renting a vehicle is a popular way to travel across Colorado, particularly if you want to visit many places or go off the beaten path. There are car rental agencies in the state's main airports and cities. The ability to explore picturesque roads, national parks, and off-the-beaten-path locations is made possible by having a vehicle.

Public Transportation: Bus and light rail services are available in Colorado's main cities, including Denver, Colorado Springs, and Boulder. It is simple to get about the Denver metropolitan region because to the Regional Transportation District (RTD), which runs a vast network of bus and light rail lines. There are public transit networks in other places as well, however the service may be less extensive.

Amtrak: Colorado is traversed by a number of Amtrak lines, the country's passenger train service. Between Chicago and San Francisco, the California Zephyr route makes stops in a number of Colorado communities, including Denver and Glenwood Springs. A lovely and relaxing way to see the state is by taking the train.

Services for Intercity Buses: A number of bus companies provide interstate travel within Colorado and links to adjacent states. Major city routes are operated by organizations like Greyhound and Bustang, offering it an affordable choice for getting between locations.

Ride-Sharing Services: For quick travels within cities, ride-sharing services like Uber and Lyft are readily accessible in Colorado's largest cities.

Mountain Transportation: There are shuttle services and transportation choices accessible to well-known ski resorts and outdoor sites if you want to visit Colorado's mountainous areas. These services, which provide transportation between airports, cities, and ski slopes, often run during the winter ski season.

Walking and bicycling are both encouraged in Colorado's towns and communities, which often include well-maintained walkways and bike lanes. Walking and biking are common ways to move about cities, particularly in locations like Denver and Boulder where there are bike-sharing programs and large trail networks.

Consider considerations like your location, the length of your stay, the degree of comfort and flexibility you desire, and the particular activities and places you want to explore when selecting transportation alternatives in Colorado. Additionally, it's crucial to monitor for any changes to transportation options or routes, particularly during periods of high travel demand or in reaction to unforeseeable circumstances.

Options for Accommodations

Numerous lodging options are available in Colorado to accommodate a variety of tastes and price ranges. The state offers a wide range of possibilities, whether you're looking for luxurious lodgings, warm mountain cabins, affordable solutions, or unusual places to stay.

Here are a few well-liked lodging choices in Colorado:

Hotels & Resorts: Colorado is home to a wide variety of hotels and resorts, from opulent places to affordable choices. Numerous hotels catering to different requirements and interests are available in major towns including Denver, Colorado Springs, and Aspen. Mountain resorts provide access to outdoor activities and breathtaking scenery.

Bed & Breakfasts: For those looking for a more private and intimate encounter, bed and 🔍 are a beautiful choice. Colorado's bed & breakfasts provide cozy lodging, delicious breakfasts, and individualized hospitality. They are often found in historic buildings or beautiful landscapes.

Vacation rentals: Families and bigger groups often choose to rent a vacation house, condo, or cabin in Colorado. For individuals who want more room and solitude when traveling, vacation rentals provide all the conveniences of home and often come furnished with all the facilities.

Ranches and Guest Ranches: Since Colorado has a rich history of ranching, staying at one of the state's ranches or guest ranches gives tourists the chance to really experience the cowboy lifestyle. Ranches provide chances for horseback riding, fishing, and other outdoor pursuits, with lodging options ranging from basic cabins to opulent lodges.

RV parks and campgrounds: Colorado is a fantastic place for campers because of its stunning natural surroundings. There are several campsites and RV parks in the state, ranging from developed areas with facilities to more outlying and rustic areas. There are alternatives available all around the state, including in national parks, state parks, and private campsites, whether you like tent camping, RV camping, or glamping.

Mountain lodges and cabins: The mountainous areas of Colorado are home to a wide variety of lodges, cabins, and chalets that provide a warm and private mountain refuge. These lodgings often provide breathtaking views, fireplaces, and quick access to outdoor recreation areas.

Unique Accommodations: Colorado has a variety of unique lodging alternatives for people looking for one-of-a-kind experiences. Treehouses, yurts, tipis, and even historical ghost town lodgings are available. These outlandish lodgings provide unique and interesting experiences.

It's crucial to reserve lodging well in advance, particularly during busy vacation times like the summer when national parks are visited in abundance or the winter ski season. When selecting your lodging, take into account the surroundings, features, and accessibility to activities. Check for any additional limits or criteria, such as pet-friendly lodgings or accessible amenities, according to your needs.

Luxury Inns

Here is a list of the top resorts in Colorado, along with a basic idea of their costs. Please be aware that costs might change based on the time of year, accommodation types, and availability.

Colorado Springs's The Broadmoor
$400 to $1,200 per night is the price range.

Denver's (The Ritz-Carlton, Denver)
Price per night: $300 to $800

Aspen's The Little Nell
$500 to $1,500 per night is the price range.

The Four Seasons Hotel Denver
Costs per night range from $400 to $1,000.

The Vail - Sebastian (Vail)
$400 to $1,200 per night is the price range.

Aspen's The St. Regis Aspen Resort
Price per night: between $600 and $2,000

Bachelor Gulch The Ritz-Carlton (Avon)
$500 to $1,500 per night is the price range.

A RockResort, The Arrabelle in Vail Square (Vail)
$500 to $1,500 per night is the price range.

Aspen's Hotel Jerome, An Auberge Resort
$400 to $1,200 per night is the price range.

Denver's The Brown Palace Hotel and Spa, part of the Autograph Collection
Price per night: $300 to $800

Please be aware that these pricing ranges are approximations and may change depending on the kind of accommodation, the time of year, and availability. For the most precise and recent price information, it is usually advisable to contact the particular hotel.

Affordable lodging and rates

Here is a selection of Colorado lodging options that are within a reasonable price range. Please be aware that costs might change based on the time of year, accommodation types, and availability.

Denver's Motel 6 Thornton is located.
$50 - $80 per night is the price range.

Estes Park's (Estes Park) Rodeway Inn
Cost: $60 to $100 per night

Denver's Quality Inn & Suites Denver Stapleton
Cost: $70 to $120 per night

Colorado Springs' Super 8 by Wyndham Colorado Springs/AFA Area
Cost: $60 to $100 per night

Colorado Springs' Days Inn by Wyndham Colorado Springs Airport
Cost: $60 to $100 per night

Denver's La Quinta Inn by Wyndham Denver Central
Cost: $70 to $120 per night

Denver International Airport's Baymont by Wyndham
Cost: $70 to $120 per night

Inn at Comfort Inn Estes Park
Cost: between $80 and $130 per night

Denver (Colorado Springs) Travelodge by Wyndham
Cost: $60 to $100 per night

Denver's International Airport's Econo Lodge
Cost: $60 to $100 per night

Please be aware that these pricing ranges are approximations and may change depending on the kind of accommodation, the time of year, and availability. For the most precise and recent price information, it is usually advisable to contact the particular hotel.

Guesthouses and rates that are both luxurious and affordable

Here is a selection of Colorado guesthouses that vary in price from luxurious to reasonably priced. Please be aware that costs might change based on the time of year, accommodation types, and availability.

Luxurious inns:

Pikes Peak's Cliff House (Manitou Springs)
$200 to $400 per night is the price range.

Aspen's Little Nell Residences
$500 to $1,500 per night is the price range.

Dolores' Dunton Hot Springs
Price per night: $900 to $2,000

Colorado Springs' Cloud Camp at The Broadmoor
Price per night: between $800 and $1,500

Denver's The Oxford Hotel
$200 to $400 per night is the price range.

Budget-friendly lodgings

Chalet in the mountains of Aspen
Cost: $100 to $200 per night

Evergreen's Highland Haven Creekside Inn
$150 to $300 per night is the price range.

(Silverton) Silverton Inn & Hostel
Cost: $50 to $100 per night

Cabins at Fireside Inn (Pagosa Springs)
Cost: between $80 and $150 per night

Inn at Snowberry, Crested Butte
Cost: $100 to $200 per night

Please be aware that these pricing ranges are approximations and may change depending on the kind of accommodation, the time of year, and availability. It's always a good idea to get the most recent and accurate price information directly from the particular guesthouse.

Packing list for Traveling Light and Must-Haves

It's crucial to take into account the wide variety of activities and fluctuating weather while preparing for a vacation to Colorado. Here are some suggestions for packing and a list of necessities to make sure you're ready:

Layered clothes: Since Colorado's weather is unpredictable, it's necessary to carry layers of clothes. This enables you to adapt to changes in temperature throughout the day. Include clothes like T-shirts, long sleeve shirts, sweaters or fleece, a light jacket or vest, and an outer layer that is waterproof and windproof. For outdoor activities like hiking or skiing, don't forget to bring comfortable clothing.

Comfortable Shoes: If you want to tour Colorado's national parks or hiking trails, bring a pair of comfortable walking shoes or hiking boots. A pair of sandals or flip-flops should also be packed for warmer days and leisure activities.

Outdoor Equipment: If you're thinking about participating in outdoor activities, think about bringing along the necessary supplies, such as a daypack, water bottle, hat, sunglasses, sunscreen, insect repellant, and a pair of thick socks. You could also require goods like a swimsuit, trekking poles, or snow gear depending on the season and your plans.

Travel Accessories: Keep in mind to bring travel necessities like a compact first aid kit, a reusable water bottle, a portable charger for your gadgets, and a travel adapter for your electronics.

Packing things for weather protection is essential since Colorado's weather may be erratic. Bring sun protection such as a hat or cap, a poncho or light rain gear, and a small umbrella. Bring a scarf, hat, and gloves if you're coming in the winter to remain comfortable in the chilly weather.

Toiletries, medicines, and personal care products should be brought. Don't forget to pack your toothbrush, toothpaste, shampoo, conditioner, bar soap, and any prescription drugs you may need.

Consider bringing biodegradable toiletries if you're camping or staying in a remote location.

Travel papers: Make sure all necessary travel papers are safe and convenient to access. Included in this are your passport, ID card, airline tickets, hotel bookings, hotel reservation confirmations in electronic form, and any required visas or permissions.

Bring a variety of cash and credit/debit cards with you for your financial requirements. Although most locations take credit cards, it's a good idea to have extra cash on hand in case of emergencies or smaller businesses.

gadgets: Depending on your requirements, you may want to bring gadgets like a smartphone, camera, charger, and any further equipment you may need. Don't forget to include the proper chargers or adapters for your equipment.

Pack a book, e-reader, or travel guides on Colorado to enrich your trip and give helpful information if you prefer reading or need amusement while traveling.

Don't forget to pack for the exact things you want to do and the time of year you'll be there. Before traveling to Colorado, check the weather prediction to make sure you have the right clothes and equipment packed. A reusable bag may be useful for transporting necessities on day excursions or for shopping.

Exploring Denver

Learning about the Mile High City

Due to its height of 5,280 feet (1,609 meters), Denver, often known as the Mile High City, provides a bustling metropolitan experience against an incredible background of natural beauty. When exploring Denver, keep these highlights and activities in mind:

Walking around downtown Denver is a good way to start your tour of the area. Visit the lively 16th Street Mall, which is dotted with stores, eateries, and entertainment options. Take time to see the city's colorful street art and old buildings.

Visit Museums and Cultural institutions: There are several museums and cultural institutions in Denver. The Denver Museum of Nature & Science has intriguing exhibitions on science, natural history, and the indigenous cultures of the area, while the Denver Art Museum displays a remarkable collection of artwork. The Clyfford Still Museum, which showcases the works of the famous abstract expressionist artist, should not be missed.

Denver has a vibrant craft beer sector with many breweries to visit. Enjoy the Craft Breweries and Food sector. Visit the vibrant areas of RiNo (River North Art District) and LoHi (Lower Highlands) to taste local brews, or go on a brewery tour. Denver also has a dynamic food scene with a broad variety of dining alternatives, including food trucks and farm-to-table establishments.

Experience Sports and Outdoor Recreation: Attend a game and support the neighborhood teams since Denver is a sports-mad city. The Denver Broncos (NFL), Colorado Rockies (MLB), Denver Nuggets (NBA), and Colorado Avalanche (NHL) are just a few of the professional sports teams that call this city home. Rock climbing, biking, and other outdoor pursuits are available in the beautiful Rocky Mountains nearby for adventurers.

Discover Historic communities: Denver is home to a number of interesting historic communities. Experience the Victorian architecture, boutique stores, and fine dining establishments of Larimer Square, Denver's oldest block. Beautiful views of the city skyline are combined with quaint shops, hip restaurants, and other attractions in the Highland area.

Discover the Denver Botanic Gardens: Get away from the bustle of the city and spend some time relaxing at the Denver Botanic Gardens. A wide variety of plant collections, including themed gardens, conservatories, and works of art, are shown in this paradise. Walk gently around the grounds and take in the tranquil atmosphere.

Visit Red Rocks Park and Amphitheatre: Located just outside of Denver, Red Rocks Park is home to a stunning red sandstone amphitheater. Visit a performance in the renowned outdoor amphitheater, noted for its breath-taking vistas and first-rate acoustics, or go for a trek along the park's trails.

Discover the Denver Zoo and Denver Aquarium: The Denver Zoo, which is home to a diverse range of animals from throughout the globe, is a great place for family-friendly excursions. The Downtown Aquarium provides an immersive underwater experience with displays of marine life and interactive exhibits.

Enjoy Art and Music events: Throughout the year, Denver is home to a number of art and music events. A few examples of the city's thriving cultural events are the Underground Music Showcase, Denver

Chalk Art Festival, and Cherry Creek Arts Festival.

Day excursions: Arrange day excursions to surrounding locations to take advantage of Denver's closeness to natural treasures. Discover picturesque driving, hiking trails, and animal watching at Rocky Mountain National Park. Take a tour of Georgetown, a former mining town, or try white-water rafting on the Arkansas River.

Denver has a wide range of attractions and activities to enthrall tourists, whether they are interested in the arts and culture, outdoor activities, or just taking in the local flavor.

Famous Places and Attractions

Numerous well-known sites and attractions in Colorado serve to highlight the state's natural beauty, history, and cultural legacy. Here are a few places you really must see:

Rocky Mountain National Park is a stunning natural beauty that is situated just northwest of Denver. Through picturesque drives, hiking paths, and animal watching, discover its breathtaking peaks, alpine lakes, and unique ecosystems.

Garden of the Gods is a breathtaking geological structure with soaring red rock formations, and it is located near Colorado Springs. Take in the magnificent views of the surroundings while hiking and rock climbing.

Find out more about Mesa Verde National Park's historic cliff houses and archaeological sites. Learn about the elaborate cliff homes carved out of sandstone cliffs, one of the well-preserved examples of the ancient Puebloan civilisation.

Pikes Peak: Also referred to as America's Mountain, Pikes Peak rises 14,115 feet (4,302 meters) above sea level and provides stunning vistas from its top. Drive, ride the cog train, or, for the more daring, trek the beautiful paths to the summit.

Experience the rush of crossing the Royal Gorge Bridge, one of the tallest suspension bridges in the world, which spans the magnificent Royal Gorge. Take a zip line adventure, ride the aerial tram, or just take in the breathtaking views of the untamed canyon.

Marvel at the enormous sand dunes perched against the Sangre de Cristo Mountains at the Great Sand Dunes National Park and Preserve. Explore the park's different ecosystems or take a hike or sled ride down the sandy slopes.

Visit the stunning Black Canyon of the Gunnison National Park to take in its strikingly small size, sheer cliffs, and dark, constricting depths. Hike the trails, take a beautiful drive along the South Rim Road, or take in the stunning views from the rim.

Discover the historic Union Station in Denver, a stunningly renovated transit hub and architectural wonder. Take advantage of the area's boutiques, eateries, and pubs or take a train to one of the many Colorado locations.

Colorado State Capitol: Marvel at the magnificent neoclassical design of the Colorado State Capitol in Denver. Visit the rotunda for sweeping views of the city and the Rocky Mountains and take a guided tour to learn about the history of the state.

Visit the Denver Museum of Nature & Science to immerse yourself in science displays, space exploration, and natural history. The museum provides interesting activities for people of all ages, including a planetarium and dinosaur fossils.

These are just a handful of Colorado's famous attractions and sites. The state provides a variety of places to visit and make special memories, whether you're enthralled by natural beauties, interested by history, or intrigued by cultural riches.

Cultural and Creative Pleasures

Colorado has a diverse array of museums, galleries, theaters, and festivals, making it a thriving center for cultural and creative pleasures. Here are some of the best creative and cultural attractions to check out:

Denver Art Museum: The Denver Art Museum, which is based in Denver, is well-known for its extensive collection of works spanning many different art genres and civilizations. Explore historical relics, current and modern pieces of art, and exhibitions of famous artists' work.

The Clyfford Still Museum, located in Denver, is devoted to the life and artistic creations of abstract expressionist painter Clyfford Still. Discover Still's expressive and dramatic paintings in a location created especially for them.

Denver Performing Arts Complex: The Denver Performing Arts Complex is one of the biggest performing arts venues in the country and is home to a variety of theatrical productions, including Broadway plays, ballet, opera, and symphony concerts.

This multimodal arts facility in Colorado Springs incorporates a museum, theater, and art school. It is located at Colorado College. View a live performance, peruse the American art collection, or take part in seminars and courses for creating art.

The Telluride Film Festival is an annual event that draws well-known directors, business leaders, and movie buffs to the gorgeous mountain town of Telluride. Take in panel discussions, screenings of cutting-edge movies, and other special events.

Experience Colorado's thriving art culture during First Friday Art Walks, especially in Denver's Art District on Santa Fe and RiNo (River North Art District). Every month on the first Friday, galleries and studios open their doors to the public and host art exhibits, live music performances, and cuisine events.

Colorado Ballet: The Colorado Ballet presents world-class ballet productions that combine traditional works with cutting-edge choreography. The group puts on shows in Denver that combine fascinating narrative with gifted dancers.

Enjoy the captivating sounds of the Colorado Symphony as they play a wide range of musical genres, from pop and movie soundtrack performances to classical symphonies. In Denver's concert venues, feel the impact of live symphonic music.

Street Art: With brilliant murals covering the walls of buildings and alleyways, Colorado is renowned for its thriving street art culture. Discover beautiful street art produced by regional and international artists by strolling through areas like Denver's RiNo or Santa Fe's Art District.

events: Throughout the year, Colorado is home to a wide variety of cultural and artistic events. While the Colorado Shakespeare Festival in Boulder includes open-air productions of Shakespearean plays, the Cherry Creek Arts Festival in Denver features works by renowned artists. The Breckenridge International Festival of Arts, the Vail Dance Festival, and the Durango Bluegrass Meltdown are a few further noteworthy events.

These creative and cultural treasures of Colorado provide a venue for expression, creativity, and an appreciation of many art forms. Get involved in the state's cultural scene to see the variety of skills and experiences that make Colorado a refuge for the arts.

Outdoor Recreation and Activities

Thanks to its breathtaking landscapes, towering mountains, and extensive wilderness regions, Colorado is known for its abundance of outdoor leisure possibilities. The following are some of the best outdoor pursuits and leisure alternatives in Colorado:

Hiking & Backpacking: Colorado has a wide variety of hiking paths for all levels of experience thanks to its many national parks, state parks, and wilderness regions. Hikers may discover beautiful panoramas, alpine meadows, and clear lakes as they go along picturesque paths like Hanging Lake near Glenwood Springs or up difficult summits like Longs Peak in Rocky Mountain National Park.

Skiing and snowboarding: Skiers and snowboarders from all over the globe go to Colorado to partake in these winter activities. World-class ski resorts, including Aspen, Vail, Breckenridge, and

Telluride, are located in the state and provide diverse terrain, deep snow, and first-rate amenities.

Kayaking and Whitewater Rafting: Colorado's rivers provide exhilarating whitewater rafting adventures. Rapids on the Arkansas River, Clear Creek, and Animas River are ideal for both novice and expert paddlers, making them popular locations for thrilling rafting excursions.

Mountain riding: By going on mountain bike excursions, you may explore the rocky landscape of Colorado on two wheels. Discover a network of routes with a variety of scenery, from gorgeous rides along the Colorado Trail to difficult downhill tracks at ski resorts like Winter Park.

Rock Climbing: Colorado provides fantastic rock climbing chances with its stunning cliffs, granite formations, and towering peaks. A variety of climbing routes are available in places including Eldorado Canyon State Park, Boulder Canyon, and Garden of the Gods for both novice and expert climbers.

Colorado is a fishing enthusiast's dream because of the diversity of fish species that call its rivers, lakes, and reservoirs home. For a chance to reel in trout and other prize catches, cast your line in places like the Arkansas River, Blue Mesa Reservoir, or the Gold Medal waters of the Fryingpan River.

Camping: Spend a night in the wilds of Colorado to appreciate their magnificence. There are many locations to pitch a tent or park an RV and get close to nature, from well-known campsites to remote spots.

animals viewing: A wide variety of animals, including elk, deer, bighorn sheep, black bears, and several bird species, may be found across Colorado. To see these majestic animals in their native habitats, go to national parks and wildlife refuges like Rocky Mountain National Park or the Great Sand Dunes National Park.

Natural hot springs are abundant throughout Colorado, offering the ideal setting for rejuvenation and relaxation. For a relaxing bath in beautiful settings, visit locations like Glenwood Hot Springs, Strawberry Park Hot Springs, or Ouray Hot Springs.

Scenic Drives: Take scenic drives to see the breathtaking landscapes of Colorado. The San Juan Skyway, Trail Ridge Road, and the Million Dollar Highway all provide access to lovely communities as well as breath-taking panoramas and winding mountain routes.

Visitors may immerse themselves in the state's natural splendor, push their physical limits, and embark on life-changing outdoor experiences thanks to Colorado's outdoor pursuits and leisure possibilities. To protect the environment, always put safety first, plan ahead, and adhere to the Leave No Trace philosophy.

Price range, location of dining and nightlife

In Colorado, there are many different dining and nightlife alternatives, with a broad range of prices and locations to suit a variety of tastes and budgets. Here is a summary of the various pricing points and well-liked areas:

Options that are affordable

Food trucks are ubiquitous in Colorado and provide a wide range of reasonably priced and delectable alternatives. In well-known locations like Denver's Civic Center Park or Fort Collins' Old Town Square, keep an eye out for gatherings of food trucks.

Casual Restaurants: Look into nearby casual restaurants that provide meals at affordable prices. There are several inexpensive eating alternatives in places like Boulder's Pearl Street Mall and the downtown district of Colorado Springs.

Medium-Term Options:

Neighborhood Restaurants: Colorado has a wide variety of quaint, affordable restaurants in many different communities. A variety of eating alternatives are available in places like Colorado Springs' Old Colorado City and Denver's LoDo (Lower Downtown).

Dining at breweries and pubs: Colorado is well-known for its craft beer sector, and many breweries and brewpubs provide high-quality cuisine as well. There are several breweries and

restaurants in places like Denver's RiNo area and Fort Collins' Brewery Row.
upscale dining

Gourmet food and exquisite dining experiences are available at a number of upmarket restaurants in Colorado's main cities, including Denver, Boulder, and Aspen. Look for highly regarded eateries like Larimer Square in downtown Denver or Aspen's well-known eating district.
Nightlife:

Downtown areas: The Pearl Street Mall in Boulder, the Old Town Square in Fort Collins, and Downtown Denver are all well-known hotspots for nightlife. These locations provide a variety of pubs, clubs, and live music venues to suit various preferences and price ranges.
Speakeasies and bars that specialize in mixology are opening up in areas like Denver and Colorado Springs, contributing to the state of Colorado's

expanding artisan cocktail sector. For distinctive cocktail experiences, visit places like Denver's LoHi (Lower Highlands) or Colorado Springs' downtown.

It's crucial to remember that costs might change based on the particular restaurant, pub, or location. In addition, rates in affluent and touristic neighborhoods are often greater than in nearby neighborhood joints. It is advised to verify internet reviews, menus, and pricing details before visiting a certain establishment to make sure it fits your tastes and price range.

Rocky Mountain National Park

Rocky Mountain National Park overview

North-central Colorado's Rocky Mountain National Park is a stunning natural marvel and a refuge for outdoor lovers. The park, which spans more than 415 square miles (1,075 square kilometers) of rough wilderness, provides breathtaking scenery, an abundance of species, and a variety of recreational activities. An overview of Rocky Mountain National Park is provided below:

Beautiful scenery: Rocky Mountain National Park is well-known for its breathtaking mountain views, immaculate alpine lakes, lush meadows, and deep forests. Longs Peak, the park's highest peak at 14,259 feet (4,346 meters), is one of 60 summits in the area that rise beyond 12,000 feet (3,600 meters). The Colorado River meanders and the stunning cliffs, cascading waterfalls, and renowned alpine landscapes are all visible to tourists.

The park provides a vast network of paths for hiking and backpacking, ranging from leisurely strolls to strenuous alpine excursions. Over 350 miles (560 kilometers) of trails are available for hikers to explore, including the well-known routes to Alberta Falls, Bear Lake, and Emerald Lake. Longs Peak offers a strenuous summit walk with stunning panoramic views for experienced hikers.

Viewing species: Rocky Mountain National Park is a haven for a wide variety of species. Elk, mule deer, bighorn sheep, black bears, coyotes, and a wide variety of bird species may be seen by visitors. The park is also well-known for its herd of gorgeous elk, especially during the autumn rutting season when observers may see bugling sounds and impressive displays.

Scenic routes: The park has a number of scenic routes that provide access to breathtaking panoramas and chances to observe animals. As it goes through the park and rises to a height of 12,183 feet (3,713 meters), Trail Ridge Road—the highest continuously paved road in North America—offers stunning views of the mountains and alpine tundra in the area.

Rocky Mountain National Park has a number of campsites that are suitable for tent and RV camping. Backcountry camping offers a more immersive experience, while constructed campsites with facilities are available to visitors. The park has several picnic spaces that provide picturesque locations for eating in the great outdoors.

Photography and wildlife observation: The park's scenic surroundings provide a never-ending supply of picture possibilities. Photographers and nature lovers may get up close and personal with the park's many natural delights, from photographing breathtaking scenery to finding elusive species.

Rocky Mountain National area has visitor centers that provide information, displays, and educational programs on the geology, animals, and history of the area. The programs provide insights into the biological and cultural value of the park via treks, discussions, and chances to see animals under the guidance of rangers.

beautiful Activities: Rocky Mountain National Park becomes a beautiful paradise throughout the winter. Snowshoeing, cross-country skiing, and animal watching in the winter are among the activities that visitors may take part in. The park's sceneries are calm and beautiful when they are blanketed with snow.

You may take in the grandeur of the Rocky Mountains, see a variety of species, and engage in a variety of outdoor activities by visiting Rocky

Mountain National Park. For nature lovers and outdoor enthusiasts alike, this national park provides an exceptional experience, whether you're looking for adventure, calmness, or a closer connection with nature.

Wildlife and the Natural Wonders

The amazing variety and picturesque landscapes of Colorado are highlighted by the state's unique species and natural treasures. The following are some of Colorado's most noteworthy wildlife and natural wonders:

Wildlife:

Elk: One of the greatest elk populations in the United States is found in Colorado. Male elk engage in theatrical displays and bugling cries during the autumn rutting season, especially in places like Rocky Mountain National Park and Estes Park.

Bighorn Sheep: The state is home to large populations of bighorn sheep in its hilly areas, such as the Rocky Mountains and the Colorado National Monument. Watch these magnificent creatures scale rocks and clash skulls during mating rituals.

Black bears: Black bears are a common sight in wooded regions across Colorado. When visiting national parks like Rocky Mountain National Park or San Juan National Forest, keep a look out for these secretive animals.

Mountain lions live in Colorado's wilderness regions, however they are seldom seen. These secretive carnivores inhabit a variety of environments, including canyons and hilly areas. If you enter their environment, use care and be mindful of your surroundings.

Birds: A broad range of bird species are drawn to Colorado's different environments. Check out the reservoirs and lakes for magnificent bald eagles, bright mountain bluebirds in wide-open meadows, and the recognizable peregrine falcons who build their nests on cliffs.

Natural marvels

The Maroon Bells are two famous mountains in the Aspen area that are encircled by lovely alpine meadows. Especially in the autumn when the aspen trees turn golden, this spectacular natural marvel provides amazing vistas and is one of Colorado's most often photographed landscapes.

Great Sand Dunes National Park and Preserve: Great Sand Dunes National Park is home to the highest sand dunes in North America. A bizarre and alluring scene is produced by the contrast of the tall sand dunes and the Sangre de Cristo Mountains.

Garden of the Gods: A natural marvel with imposing red rock formations, Garden of the Gods is located near

Colorado Springs. Take use of the park's pathways to see the magnificent rock formations and enjoy sweeping views of the surroundings.

Marvel at the steep cliffs and constricting depths of the Black Canyon of the Gunnison National Park. This spectacular natural marvel gives breathtaking views of the Gunnison River raging and the dark, tight canyon.

Hanging Lake: A hidden jewel with turquoise waters that are crystal pure and a magnificent cascade, Hanging Lake is located in Glenwood Canyon. The unusual travertine structures around the lake provide a mystical and peaceful ambiance.

Visit the Royal canyon in the vicinity of Caon City, where the Arkansas River created a profound and constricting canyon. Experience the excitement of a zip line adventure, the adrenaline of a trip on the Royal Gorge Railroad, or the stunning views from the suspension bridge.

Incredible chances for exploration, photography, and enjoyment of Colorado's natural beauty are provided by its animals and other natural treasures. To protect these priceless ecosystems for future generations, keep in mind to respect animals, abide by park rules, and use Leave No Trace principles.

Trails for hiking and scenic drives

Numerous hiking paths and scenic routes are available in Colorado, showcasing the state's breathtaking scenery and unspoiled beauty. Here are some noteworthy possibilities, whether you're looking for a relaxing trek or a breath-taking drive:

hiking routes

Hanging Lake: This well-known hike in Glenwood Canyon leads to a stunning turquoise lake perched precariously above a rock. Despite the trail's moderate difficulty, hikers are rewarded with breathtaking vistas and a flowing cascade.

Explore the distinctive rock formations and striking vistas of this Colorado Springs park, Garden of the Gods. Visitors may enjoy the varied challenges of the hiking paths while taking in the expansive vistas and towering red rocks.

The Maroon Bells-Snowmass Wilderness, which is close to Aspen, has a number of hiking paths for hikers of all skill levels. The Maroon Bells, two imposing peaks that reflect in a crystal-clear alpine lake, may be seen from the Maroon Lake Scenic Trail in picture-perfect fashion.

Rocky Mountain National Park: The park's more than 350 miles (560 kilometers) of trails provide a wide range of hiking opportunities. Hikers may discover alpine meadows, glacial basins, and stunning panoramas on routes ranging from the easy Bear Lake Loop to the strenuous climb up Longs Peak.

Great Sand Dunes National Park: At the Great Sand Dunes, you may go on a unique hiking adventure while admiring snow-capped mountains in the distance. Popular options include the High Dune Trail and the Medano Creek Trail.

enticing drives

Trail Ridge Road: This well-known road in Rocky Mountain National Park ascends to altitudes of more than 12,000 feet (3,600 meters), providing breathtaking vistas of alpine meadows, craggy peaks, and animal sightings. The seasonal road links Estes Park with Grand Lake.

San Juan Skyway: This 236-mile (380-kilometer) circle travels across southwest Colorado's San Juan Mountains and offers stunning views of the range's mountains, valleys, old mining towns, and the fabled Million Dollar Highway.

Independence Pass: At a height of 12,095 feet (3,687 meters), this picturesque road crosses the Continental Divide. It provides sweeping views of the surrounding peaks and alpine beauty and links Aspen to Twin Lakes.

The Million Dollar Highway is a portion of U.S. Route 1 that passes through the San Juan Mountains. The stunning scenery and exhilarating twists of Route 550 are well recognized. You pass through charming villages like Ouray and Silverton on the way.

Pikes Peak Highway: Take this beautiful road to the top of Pikes Peak, one of Colorado's well-known fourteeners. Observe the surrounding landscapes from a sweeping perspective, including Colorado Springs and the Eastern Plains.

You can immerse yourself in Colorado's natural beauties, from soaring peaks and tranquil lakes to dramatic canyons and unusual rock formations, on these hiking routes and scenic drives. Before hiking, always check the path for conditions and closures, and come equipped with the right equipment and safety measures.

Adventures in the Backcountry and Camping

In Colorado, camping and backcountry excursions are common pastimes that allow you to fully immerse yourself in the state's breathtaking natural landscapes and enjoy the great outdoors. Here is a list of camping possibilities and wilderness excursions in Colorado:

Camping choices

Numerous established campsites may be found throughout Colorado's state parks, national forests, and other public areas. Typically, these campsites have facilities like picnic tables, fire rings, bathrooms, and sometimes showers. A couple of well-liked choices include Chatfield State Park close to Denver and Moraine Park Campground in Rocky Mountain National Park.

RV camping is available in Colorado, with a variety of sites with water, power, and sewage connections. There are approved RV sites in many established campsites, as well as private RV parks and resorts spread out over the state. Popular locations for RV camping include Cherry Creek State Park in Aurora and St. Vrain State Park close to Longmont.

scattered Camping: Many national forests and Bureau of Land Management (BLM) regions allow scattered camping for a more rural experience. You may pitch up tent in specified locations without facilities when you go dispersed camping. It's crucial to observe Leave No Trace guidelines and be informed of any local limits or legislation.

Backcountry Camping: For those looking for a more quiet and remote experience, Colorado has several excellent backcountry camping options. In certain places, such wilderness zones or high-alpine regions, permits could be necessary. To reduce effect, learn about particular areas and rules ahead of time and follow Leave No Trace guidelines.

Backcountry Explorations

Backpacking: There are many chances for backpacking experiences in Colorado thanks to the state's large route network and wilderness regions. The Colorado Trail, Continental Divide Trail, and Indian Peaks Wilderness are a few well-known backpacking locations. Before starting a backpacking trip, research the route conditions, permits, and safety issues.

Colorado is known for its magnificent peaks and exhilarating climbing opportunities for expert climbers. Climbers are drawn to mountains like Longs Peak, Capitol Peak, and Maroon Bells because of their difficult routes and magnificent summit vistas. Safety depends on having the right tools, abilities, and understanding of climbing tactics.

Multi-day Wilderness hikes: The Weminuche Wilderness and the Lost Creek Wilderness in Colorado are two wilderness regions that provide chances for multi-day hikes through stunning scenery. These journeys often include traversing rocky terrain, fording rivers, and camping far from civilization. For information on permits, trail conditions, and suggested routes, contact your local ranger station.

Colorado has beautiful rivers and lakes that are perfect for canoeing and kayaking excursions. For those who like kayaking, the Arkansas River, the Colorado River, and Dillon Reservoir are popular locations. If you're new to the sport, take into consideration guided tours and be mindful of water levels, rapids, and safety procedures.

When organizing camping and backcountry excursions in Colorado, learn about the particular rules, authorizations, and safety requirements for the region you want to visit. Check the weather, have your essentials close by, and let others know what you're planning. To guarantee a happy and sustainable outdoor experience, respect the environment, animals, and your fellow explorers.

Localities and Attractions

Many lovely communities and tourist destinations in Colorado provide one-of-a-kind chances to experience the state's rich culture, history, and natural beauty. The following prominent adjacent towns and tourist destinations are worth visiting:

Boulder: Known for its energetic downtown, Boulder combines outdoor adventure, cultural landmarks, and a thriving restaurant scene. Visit the gorgeous Boulder Creek Path, the well-known Pearl Street Mall, and the neighboring Flatirons for a trek.

Colorado Springs: At the foot of Pikes Peak, this vibrant city has a breathtaking natural setting. The famous Garden of the Gods, the interesting United States Air Force Academy, and the storied Manitou Springs shouldn't be missed.

Aspen is a well-known mountain resort town known for its skiing, opulent hotels, and vibrant arts community. Explore the attractive downtown area or engage in outdoor sports like skiing, snowboarding, and hiking. You can also visit the Aspen Art Museum.

Durango: Located in the state's southwest, Durango has a quaint Old

West vibe. Take a ride on the venerable Durango & Silverton Narrow Gauge Railroad, stroll along Main Avenue, and see the adjacent San Juan Mountains.

Telluride: A charming mountain town encircled by soaring peaks, Telluride is well-known for its ski slopes, music festivals, and breathtaking natural environment. Visit the historic downtown district, climb to Bridal Veil Falls, and take a gorgeous gondola ride.

Estes Park is a well-known entryway to outdoor experiences and is located near the entrance of Rocky Mountain National Park. Take in the breathtaking mountain vistas, tour the lovely downtown area, and stop at the Stanley Hotel, which served as the inspiration for Stephen King's "The Shining".

Glenwood Springs: This adventure and leisure destination is well-known for its hot springs and outdoor pursuits.

Explore Glenwood Canyon, take a relaxing bath at Glenwood Hot Springs, and go to the exhilarating Glenwood Caverns Adventure Park.

Manitou Springs: A quirky and creative town with natural mineral springs and a thriving arts culture, Manitou Springs is close to Colorado Springs. Take a look around the specialized stores, wander through the Manitou Springs Cliff Dwellings, and drink from a natural spring.

Fort Collins: Fort Collins has a lively and welcoming environment and is well-known for its craft beer culture and active downtown. Visit the Colorado State University campus, take part in some outdoor activities at Horsetooth Reservoir, and explore the breweries along the Fort Collins Ale Trail.

Ouray: Soak in the natural hot springs, explore the breathtaking Box Canyon

Falls Park, and take a picturesque drive down the Million Dollar Highway in Ouray, which is sometimes referred to as the "Switzerland of America."

These local towns and destinations provide a wide variety of activities, from leisure time and scenic beauty to outdoor discovery and cultural exploration. Every place promotes Colorado's distinct character and welcomes tourists to experience the state's great attractions.

Regions of Colorado Springs and Pikes Peak

Looking around Colorado Springs

Colorado's lively metropolis of Colorado Springs is located at the foot of the magnificent Pikes Peak. Colorado Springs has a range of experiences for tourists to enjoy with its magnificent natural surroundings and a variety of activities. The following is a guide to seeing Colorado Springs:

Garden of the Gods: The Garden of the Gods is a natural wonder with imposing red rock formations. Start your trip by exploring it. Enjoy the park's winding hiking and walking paths, or get a different viewpoint by joining a guided jeep or Segway tour.

Pikes Peak: Take the Pikes Peak Highway or the cog train to the top of Pikes Peak, one of Colorado's most recognizable fourteeners. Enjoy stunning 360-degree views of the area's landscapes, including Colorado Springs.

Manitou Springs is a lovely village in Colorado Springs that is well-known for its natural mineral springs and creative atmosphere. Visit the Manitou Incline for a strenuous trek, see the Manitou

Springs Cliff Dwellings, or peruse the distinctive boutiques and galleries along Manitou Avenue.

U.S. Air Force Academy: Travel to the U.S. Air Force Academy, which is situated in Colorado Springs. Visit the Cadet Chapel, look around the Visitor Center displays, and learn about the history and customs of the academy on a guided tour.

Olympic Training Center: At the United States Olympic Training Center, explore the world of professional athletes. Learn about the training facilities, view Olympic artifacts, and witness athletes in action by taking a guided tour.

Spend the day at the Cheyenne Mountain Zoo, which is renowned for its breathtaking mountain vistas and varied animal collection. At the Encounter Africa exhibit, you can get up close to giraffes, feed birds, and take in a variety of animal encounters and shows.

At the Colorado Springs Fine Arts Center, you may fully immerse yourself in the arts. Visit the museum's collection of American art, take in a show in the SaGaJi Theatre, and view changing exhibitions.

Visit the historic Old Colorado City, which served as the Colorado Territory's first capitol. Explore distinctive shops and galleries while strolling through brick-lined alleys, and enjoy delectable meals at neighborhood cafés and restaurants.

Explore the North Cheyenne Caon Park's natural splendor, which includes hiking trails, waterfalls, and beautiful drives. Visit the Helen Hunt Falls, climb Mount Cutler for sweeping views, or have a picnic in the serene setting.

The Colorado Springs Pioneers Museum is a great place to learn about the past of Colorado Springs and the Pikes Peak area. Discover displays that highlight the history of the city, including Native American cultures and the gold rush period.

Colorado Springs has a wide range of attractions and activities to enthrall tourists, whether they are looking for cultural experiences, outdoor adventures, or a combination of both. Enjoy the bustling atmosphere, immerse yourself in the city's fascinating history, and embrace the natural beauty of this amazing location.

The Gods' Garden

In Colorado Springs, The Garden of the Gods is a popular public park and natural monument. The park, known for its magnificent red rock formations, draws millions of tourists every year. What you should know before visiting the Garden of the Gods is as follows:

Overview: The Garden of the Gods is a National Natural Landmark and spans 1,300 acres (526 hectares) of beautiful scenery. The 300-foot-tall (91-meter) or higher sandstone formations envelop the area in awe-inspiring otherworldliness.

Visitor Center: The Garden of the Gods Visitor & Nature Center is where you should begin your journey. Through exhibits and interactive displays, you may learn about the geology, fauna, and history of the park. The facility also provides educational events, gift shops, and guided nature walks.

Hiking & Walking routes: The Garden of the Gods offers a variety of hiking and walking routes that let visitors get up close and personal with the park's distinctive structures. The wheelchair-accessible, paved Perkins Central Garden Trail offers stunning views of the granite formations. Other paths, such the Siamese Twins and Ridge, provide more difficult terrain and expansive views.

Rock Climbing: Rock climbers of all abilities frequent the park as a popular location. Advanced routes may be attempted by experienced climbers, while novices can benefit from local outfitters' guided climbing expeditions and training. Climbers must follow established zones and safety precautions, and they need permits.

Scenic Drives & Biking: Take a scenic drive along one of the park's paved roads to take in the grandeur of the Garden of the Gods. From the luxury of your car, you may enjoy fantastic views of the rock formations along the Garden

Drive and Juniper Way Loop. On specified park roads, biking is also allowed.

The Garden of the Gods offers a number of visitor facilities to make your trip more enjoyable. Throughout the park, picnic sites with tables and grills are accessible so that you may eat outside in the breathtaking scenery. There are plenty of parking spaces accessible, as well as conveniently situated restrooms and drinking fountains.

Guided Tours: Take a guided tour of the Garden of the Gods for a more in-depth experience. Insightful guides may provide intriguing details about the geology, history, and Native American links of the area. Popular choices include Segway excursions, Jeep tours, and electric bike rides.

The Garden of the Gods provides several possibilities for photography lovers to see wildlife. Photograph the stunning rock formations with the Colorado scenery in the background. A variety of bird species, mule deer, rabbits, foxes, and other animals should be on your radar as well.

Special activities and Programs: The Garden of the Gods organizes a number of activities and programs all year long, including led walks, educational talks, and workshops that emphasize nature. For the most recent details on planned activities, check the park's website or visitor center.

Accessibility: The Garden of the Gods works hard to make all visitors as accessible as possible. Wheelchair-accessible facilities, paved walkways, and accessible parking are all provided. Resources for guests with impairments are also available at the visitor center.

For individuals who like the outdoors, are nature lovers, or are searching for breathtaking natural beauty, The Garden of the Gods is a must-visit location. The park's extraordinary and stunning granite formations will make a lasting impact whether you decide to trek, climb, or just enjoy the views.

Pikes Peak: The Mountain of America

Pikes mountain, sometimes known as "America's Mountain," is a well-known and recognizable mountain situated close to Colorado Springs. At 14,115 feet (4,302 meters) above sea level, it provides stunning panoramic views and a variety of outdoor activities. What you should know before visiting Pikes Peak is as follows:

Pikes Peak Highway: Traveling via the Pikes Peak Highway is the most well-liked method of getting to the peak. From the base to the top, a picturesque toll road that is 19 miles (31 km) long winds through meadows, woods, and spectacular alpine scenery. There are many opportunities to stop and take in the scenery as you go.

Consider taking a trip on the Pikes Peak Cog Railway for an unusual and interesting adventure. Since it has been running since 1891, this cogwheel train provides a thrilling trip to the peak. As the train ascends over rocky terrain and reaches the summit, take in the expansive vistas.

Barr Trail: You may walk the Barr Trail to the peak if you're looking for a more challenging alternative. The length of this difficult trek is 13 miles (21 kilometers), and it rises 2,255 meters (7,400 feet) in elevation. Due to its length and certain steep portions, it is suggested for experienced hikers only. Plan ahead, carry the right equipment, and be ready for shifting weather conditions.

Summit House: The Summit House, a tourist center with services including bathrooms, a gift shop, and a restaurant, is located at the summit of Pikes Peak. During your break, have some food and take in the stunning panoramas of the nearby mountains and valleys.

Possibilities for Photography: Pikes Peak offers breathtaking photographic chances all along the route. Capture the distinctive alpine flora and animals, panoramic vistas, and shifting landscapes. Photographers will find a variety of interesting vistas on the mountain, from brilliant wildflowers in the summer to snow-capped summits in the winter.

Outdoor Activities: There are several outdoor activities to enjoy in Pikes Peak. You may go hiking, mountain biking, or fishing in surrounding lakes and streams throughout the summer. Snowboarding, skiing, and snowshoeing are popular winter activities that draw tourists to the mountain at this time.

The Pikes Peak base and summit both have gift stores where you may purchase souvenirs. You may discover a broad variety of keepsakes here to remember your trip, including apparel, literature, artwork, and one-of-a-kind souvenirs.

Weather considerations: The weather on Pikes Peak may be erratic, with temperature swings and quickly shifting circumstances. It's important to layer your clothing, pack plenty of water, food, and sunscreen. Before starting your travel, check the weather and the road conditions.

Pikes Peak Hill Climb: Held every year, the Pikes Peak International Hill Climb is a motorsport competition that draws competitors from all over the globe. Observe as accomplished drivers take on the difficult course and compete for the top spot in a range of vehicle classifications.

Visitor Information: For the most recent information on fees, road closures, and safety precautions, consult the official website before visiting Pikes Peak. Plan your journey appropriately, leaving enough time to soak in the breathtaking scenery and truly appreciate the experience.

Pikes Peak is a well-known location that provides a special experience and the ability to take in Colorado's scenic magnificence. Whether you choose to drive, ride the cog train, or trek to the top of "America's Mountain," you will be rewarded with breathtaking views and a feeling of achievement.

Train between Manitou Springs and Cog

Near Colorado Springs, Colorado, there are two interconnected attractions: Manitou Springs and the Cog Railway. What you should know before visiting Manitou Springs and riding the Cog Railway is as follows:

Manitou Springs is a lovely hamlet just west of Colorado Springs that is well-known for its natural mineral springs, creative vibe, and fascinating history. Here are some of Manitou Springs' highlights:
Mineral Springs: The town is well-known for its eight various mineral springs that are spread out around the region. Visitors are welcome to sample

and fill bottles with the mineral-rich waters, which are said to have therapeutic qualities.

The Manitou Incline is a well-liked hiking path that provides a strenuous exercise and breathtaking vistas. Over 2,744 steps and 610 meters of elevation gain are achieved on the course in little under a mile.

Manitou Avenue: Take a stroll along the town's main thoroughfare, which is packed with distinctive stores, galleries, eateries, and boutiques. Discover the local art scene, indulge in delectable food, and shop for trinkets.

Visit the Manitou Cliff Dwellings, a remarkable historical location that displays the way of life and architecture of the Ancestral Puebloans. Discover the region's Native American heritage by seeing the well-preserved cliff dwellings, going to the museum, and more.

The Pikes Peak Cog Railway is a well-known tourist destination that offers a picturesque and storied ride to the top of Pikes Peak. Here's what to anticipate:

Experience a cog train: The Pikes Peak Cog train, the tallest cog railway in the world, provides a relaxing and beautiful climb to Pikes Peak's top. You may take in panoramic vistas of the surrounding surroundings throughout the about three-hour round trip commute.

The Cog Railway has been in use since 1891 and is recognized as a historic site on the National Register of Historic Places. It gives a unique approach to appreciate Pikes Peak's splendor and is a marvel of engineering.

Views from the top include stunning panoramas of the Colorado Rockies, including far-off mountain ranges, alpine lakes, and expansive vistas. Spend some time strolling around the summit area, perusing the gift store, and taking in the breathtaking scenery.

Train Comfort: The Cog Railway offers cozy, climate-controlled train coaches to make the trip to the peak enjoyable. The unhindered views from the windows let you stop along the trip and take beautiful pictures.

You can really immerse yourself in the history, culture, and natural beauty of the area by combining a trip to Manitou Springs with a ride on the Pikes Peak Cog Railway. This combo offers a well-rounded trip in the Colorado Springs region, from perusing the distinctive stores and sampling the mineral springs in Manitou Springs to riding the cog railway to the top of Pikes Peak.

Academy of the Air Force and Museums

A special chance to study American history, customs, and accomplishments is provided by the United States Air Force Academy and the nearby museums. Aerial Force. What you should know before visiting the Air Force Academy and its museums is as follows:

The United States Air Force Academy (USAFA) is a prominent military school that educates future American officers. It is situated just north of Colorado Springs. Aerial Force. Here are some of the academy's high points:

Cadet Chapel: The Cadet Chapel, one of the academy's most recognizable buildings, is an architectural wonder with recognizable spires and lovely stained-glass windows. It is accessible to outsiders and acts as a place of prayer for cadets.

The Air Force Academy's integrity, service, and excellence are symbolized by a statue of the Winged Victory in the Honor Court, which is located in the center of the institution.

Start your tour in the visitor center where you may learn about the history, goals, and cadet experience of the school via educational exhibits and displays. Additionally, the center offers details about guided tours and other guest services.

Take a walk around the Cadet Area of the United States Air Force Academy to see the distinctive architecture and layout of the school. Admire the open areas and modernist structures created to promote cooperation, leadership, and learning.

The USAFA is renowned for its falconry program, which prepares birds of prey for use in official Academy activities and educational outreach. During your stay, you could have the opportunity to see a falconry display.

The Doolittle Hall, a building that showcases exhibitions recognizing the accomplishments of Air Force school alumni, is run by the United States Air Force Academy Association of alumni and is situated next to the school. It also holds numerous events and acts as a hub for alumni gatherings.

Athletic Facilities at the United States Air Force Academy: The USAFA is home to several remarkable athletic facilities, including the Falcon Stadium for football, the Clune Arena for basketball, and the Cadet Gym for a variety of sports. Consider going to any athletic events or contests that are taking place while you are there to see the energy and commitment of Air Force Academy athletes.

The Planetarium at the United States Air Force school provides educational shows and presentations on astronomy, space travel, and the night sky. It is a part of the school. For showtimes, see the calendar, then take in a fascinating and instructive experience.

The history of the Air Force Academy and the United States is on display in the Falcon Heritage Museum at the Air Force Academy. Aerial Force. Discover displays of antiques, memorabilia, and aircraft that illustrate the academy's contributions to the national security.

The United States' National Museum. Air Force: Although not physically housed at the Air Force Academy, the U.S. A must-see place for aviation fans is Air Force near Dayton, Ohio. The museum has a sizable collection of weapons, artifacts, and planes relevant to American history. Aerial Force.

You may learn about American commitment, discipline, and accomplishments by visiting the Air Force Academy and the museums it is home to. Aerial Force. You'll get a greater understanding of the Air Force's function in protecting the country whether you explore the academy's grounds, learn about its history, or experience the thrill of flight at the museums.

Southwestern Colorado and Mesa Verde National Park

Mesa Verde's Old Cliff Dwellings

A fascinating archaeological site, the prehistoric cliff dwellings at Mesa Verde National Park in southwest Colorado provide a window into the life and culture of the Ancestral Puebloans. What you should know before visiting Mesa Verde's historic cliff homes is as follows:

Overview: The UNESCO-designated Mesa Verde National Park is home to over 5,000 archaeological monuments, including close to 600 cliff houses. The Anasazi, also known as the Ancestral

Puebloans, lived in the region from around 600 to 1300 AD and constructed these houses.

Cliff houses: Mesa Verde's greatest draw is its cliff houses. These remarkable constructions, which vary in size from tiny one-room huts to multi-story complexes, were constructed into natural alcoves in the cliff cliffs. Cliff Palace, Balcony House, and Spruce Tree House are a few of the well-known cliff homes you may explore.

Guided Tours: You must sign up for a ranger-led tour in order to visit the cliff houses. The tours provide visitors a rare chance to enter and explore the homes while learning about its design, function, and previous occupants. The Mesa Verde Visitor and Research Center sells tickets for the tours.

Visitor Center: The Mesa Verde Visitor and Research Center, which is close to the park's entrance, is where you should begin your tour. Information on the history, archaeology, and cultural importance of the park is available here, along with displays, movies, and other media. Additionally, the visitor center offers directions, park maps, and aid with visit planning.

A deeper knowledge of the Ancestral Puebloan culture, history, and archaeological findings at Mesa Verde may be gained by visiting the Chapin Mesa Archeological Museum, which is close to the visitor center. This museum has artifacts, exhibits, and interactive displays.

overlooks & Scenic Drives: Mesa Verde provides overlooks and scenic drives that let you take in the park's breathtaking scenery and wide-open panoramas. The mesas, canyons, and distant mountains may all be seen from the overlooks along the Mesa Top Loop Road.

Mesa Verde has a number of hiking and nature routes that allow visitors to explore the park's topography, vegetation, and animals. The Spruce Canyon Trail and Petroglyph Point Trail are both well-liked options for exploring the park's natural features and viewing animals.

Far View Sites: In addition to the cliff homes, the Far View Sites region has a number of surface buildings and pit houses that provide insights into the way of life and design of the Ancestral Puebloans. Take in the sights and try to picture what it might be like to live outside of the cliff alcoves.

Preservation and conservation are highly prioritized at Mesa Verde National Park in order to protect the sensitive archaeological sites. Visitors are urged to respect everything they come across, including any buildings, artifacts, or archaeological remains, and not to touch or damage them.

Seasonal Factors: The climate of Mesa Verde changes seasonally. The park is normally accessible all year round, however during the winter, access to certain cliff homes and excursions may be restricted. For the most recent information on tour schedules and park conditions, check the park's website or get in touch with the visitor center.

It is a rare chance to go back in time and understand the rich history and cultural legacy of the Ancestral Puebloans to see the historic cliff homes at Mesa Verde. Admire the well-preserved relics of this ancient civilisation as you explore the outstanding architectural accomplishments and discover more about their way of life.

Historic Town and Scenic Train Ride in Durango

Southwest Colorado's Durango is a wonderful combination of history, natural beauty, and outdoor activities. Durango is a historic town. What you should know before visiting Durango and taking its renowned scenic train journey is as follows:

Historic Downtown Durango: Begin your tour of Durango in this neighborhood. Victorian-era structures that house shops, galleries, restaurants, and cafés along the Main Avenue. Enjoy the scenery while taking a leisurely walk and discovering the local cafés and businesses.

The Durango and Silverton Narrow Gauge Railroad, a vintage train that provides a picturesque and nostalgic trip through the majestic San Juan Mountains, is one of the primary attractions of Durango. Here is what to anticipate:

Train Ride: From Durango to the storied mining town of Silverton, travel 45 miles (72 kilometers) by antique steam-powered train. Experience the pleasure of riding on a vintage railway as you take in the rhythmic chugging of the train, the breathtaking mountain landscape, and both.

Scenic Beauty: The train trip passes through gushing waterfalls, towering rock faces, and tucked-away valleys. Enjoy the untamed scenery as you immerse yourself in the rough beauty of the San Juan Mountains.

Narration and Guides: Skilled guides give narration during the trip, outlining the history, geology, and folklore of the area. Discover the history of the region's mining industry, the building of the railroad, and the difficulties experienced by the first residents.

Optional Stops: Before resuming your trip, you may get off the train at gorgeous locations like the Cascade Wye and the Elk Park turnaround to snap pictures and stretch your legs.

Durango is located along the Animas River, and the Animas River Trail offers fantastic outdoor leisure opportunities. This riverside paved route offers beautiful vistas, picnic areas, and space for biking, running, or strolling.

Mesa Verde National Park: Although not directly near Durango, Mesa Verde National Park is accessible by car. Take a day excursion to see the breathtaking archaeological sites that highlight the region's rich history, visit the old cliff dwellings, and discover more about the ancestors' Puebloan culture.

Outdoor Recreation: Durango is a mecca for nature lovers. There are many possibilities to appreciate nature and partake in exciting sports, from hiking and mountain biking in the adjacent San Juan National Forest to whitewater rafting on the Animas River.

The Durango and Silverton Railroad Museum is a worthwhile stop to make either before or after your train journey. The museum, which is close to the railway station, displays a variety of vintage locomotives, rolling equipment, and artifacts that illustrate the development of the railroad and its effects on the local community.

Cultural Events and Festivals: Throughout the year, Durango offers a number of cultural events and festivals that highlight the town's thriving arts, music, and culinary scenes. To discover whether any festivals or other noteworthy events will overlap with your visit, check the local events calendar.

Colorado's intriguing location, Durango, is made appealing by its historic allure, gorgeous train trip, and accessibility to outdoor experiences. Discover the town's fascinating history, take in the surrounding scenery, and spend an enjoyable time riding the Durango and Silverton Narrow Gauge Railroad.

Monument at the Four Corners

The only place in the nation where four states—Arizona, Colorado, New Mexico, and Utah—meet geographically is marked by the Four Corners Monument, a special landmark in the southwest of the country. What you should know before visiting the Four Corners Monument is as follows:

Geographic Location: The Navajo Nation Reservation, especially the Colorado Plateau, is where the Four

Corners Monument is located. It is around 6.8 miles (11 km) north of the Arizona town of Teec Nos Pos.

At the monument, you may simultaneously be standing in four separate states. The exact location of the intersection of the four state borders is marked with a granite disk buried in the ground as part of the monument. Walking around the disk will change the states of each limb.

Cultural Significance: Several Native American tribes, including the Navajo, Ute, Hopi, and Zuni, have ties to the Four Corners area. Native American craftsmen may be found selling jewelry, handicrafts, and traditional artwork close to the monument since the region has a strong Native American past.

The Navajo Nation manages the Four Corners Monument, which provides amenities and services to improve the tourist experience. These consist of:

Monument Plaza: A plaza area with paved pathways, seats, and shade structures surrounds the monument. Visitors may so explore and take pictures of the region in comfort.

Cultural Displays: Near the monument, local artists often erect stalls to display their handmade goods. You may see demonstrations of weaving, pottery-making, and other traditional crafts, as well as buy genuine Native American goods.

Tribal Vendors: Near the monument, you may find people selling pottery, jewelry, carpets, and other distinctive wares made by the local Native Americans.

Photo Possibilities: People often stand in various positions while taking pictures, or they put their hands and feet on the stone disk. For these picture ops, there are specific signs and lines to direct tourists.

Accessibility: There is a cost to enter the Four Corners Monument, which must be paid on-site. The monument's hours of operation change seasonally but are always open. Plan your visit appropriately since the monument is situated in a rural region and access routes may be dirt or unpaved.

Surrounding Scenery and Attractions: While the Four Corners Monument is the major draw, the area around it is home to beautiful natural scenery and other attractions. Mesa Verde National Park, Hovenweep National Monument, Monument Valley Navajo Tribal Park, and Canyon de Chelly National Monument are some of the nearby attractions. To experience the region's natural beauty and cultural legacy, think about include these places on your itinerary.

The Four Corners Monument is a special place where you may stand at the meeting point of four states and take in the diversity of the local culture. Explore the Four Corners region while taking in the panoramic vistas, interacting with regional craftspeople, and appreciating the importance of this geographical landmark.

National Monument Canyons of the Ancients

Southwest Colorado is home to the fascinating and historically important Canyons of the Ancients National Monument. What you should know before visiting the Canyons of the Ancients National Monument is as follows:

Location: The Montezuma and Dolores counties in southwest Colorado are home to the Canyons of the Ancients National Monument. It is administered by the Bureau of Land Management (BLM) and spans a sizable area of more than 176,000 acres (71,000 hectares).

Cultural Heritage: The monument's many prehistoric Puebloan cliff houses, rock art, and archaeological sites are what gave it its name. One of the largest densities of archaeological sites in the country may be found here, offering important insights into the way of life and culture of the Ancestral Puebloans who lived in the area more than a thousand years ago.

Visitor Center: The Canyons of the Ancients Visitor Center and Museum, which is close to the town of Dolores, is where you should start your trip. The center has exhibits, interactive displays, and educational activities that provide a summary of the cultural and environmental resources of the monument. A knowledgeable staff member can help you organize your trip and provide you information on the trails that are available and the current weather.

Numerous archaeological sites, including cliff houses, ancient settlements, petroglyphs, and pictographs, may be found inside the monument. While some locations allow for self-directed investigation by visitors, others need special access or guided excursions in order to preserve their fragile nature. For information on particular locations and any access limitations, contact the tourist center.

Hiking & paths: Visitors may explore the different landscapes and ancient sites of Canyons of the Ancients via a number of hiking paths. The Sand Canyon Trail, Lowry Pueblo Trail, Painted Hand Pueblo Trail, and Escalante Pueblo Trail are a few of the well-known paths. Every path provides different experiences, from historic sites to breathtaking vistas.

Viewing of Rock Art: The monument is well-known for its petroglyphs and pictographs made by the Ancestral Puebloans. These old pieces of art may be seen and appreciated in a few locations inside the monument. To protect the rock art for future generations, always treat it with care and don't touch or damage it.

Canyons of the Ancients National Monument has picturesque roads that provide breathtaking views of the surrounding surroundings. Red-rock canyons, mesas, and expansive panoramas may be seen along the scenic drives in McElmo Canyon and West Canyon, which are both highly recommended.

species and Natural Beauty: The monument is home to a variety of species and beautiful natural surroundings in addition to its archaeological riches. Watch out for animals including mule deer, coyotes, raptors, and several kinds of birds. As you visit the monument, take in the unusual geological formations, wildflowers, and vast panoramas.

Recreational camping is available in Canyons of the Ancients for those who want to prolong their stay. The monument contains designated campsites with minimal amenities, and in certain locations, wilderness camping is also allowed. Within the monument, you are permitted to do mountain biking, horseback riding, and fishing.

Visitor guidelines: It's crucial to respect and preserve the natural environment and ancient sites while visiting Canyons of the Ancients. Observe the Leave No

Trace guidelines, remain on established pathways, and refrain from touching or causing any damage to any buildings or artifacts. To maintain the area's historical and ecological integrity, leave it as you found it.

You get a rare chance to fully immerse yourself in the area's ancient history and cultural heritage by exploring Canyons of the Ancients National Monument. Explore the ruins of an intriguing civilisation, take in the breathtaking scenery, and

San Juan Skyway Scenic Byway

Southwest Colorado's San Juan Skyway Scenic Byway is a world-famous scenic route that is stunningly gorgeous. It is a 236-mile (380-kilometer) circle that travels through the breathtaking San Juan Mountains and provides access to a variety of outdoor recreational possibilities as well as spectacular vistas and quaint mountain communities. What you should know before traveling the San Juan Skyway Scenic Byway is as follows:

Route and Highlights: The Durango, Colorado, town of Durango serves as the start and terminus of the loop-shaped San Juan Skyway. It travels through a number of notable locations along the route, including:

Start your adventure in Durango, a historic city renowned for its Old West charm and for being the starting point of the Durango and Silverton Narrow Gauge Railroad.

Durango to Silverton: The first portion of the journey takes you from Durango to Silverton in the north. The breathtaking mountain vistas and the old narrow-gauge train that runs beside the road make this section particularly well-known.

Discover the little village of Silverton, which is tucked away in a lovely mountain valley. Visit the nearby stores and galleries, take in the Victorian architecture, and learn about the town's mining history.

From Silverton, follow the byway as it winds through the stunning Uncompahgre Gorge toward the town of Ouray, which is referred to as the "Switzerland of America." Marvel at the towering cliffs, cascading waterfalls, and the Million Dollar Highway, a section of the byway renowned for its scenic beauty.

Ouray: Visit the tiny town of Ouray to relax in the on-site hot springs, stroll along the quaint Main Street, and take in the breathtaking mountain views.

From Ouray to Telluride: The byway ascends and crosses Red Mountain Pass, providing stunning vistas of the surrounding peaks, as soon as you leave Ouray. Enter the charming town of Telluride, which is recognized for its world-class skiing, outdoor activities, and thriving arts scene. Telluride is located in a box canyon.

From Telluride to Dolores: As you travel south towards the town of Dolores, the byway travels through picturesque mountain passes, alpine forests, and wide lowlands.

Dolores to Durango: From Dolores, you make your way back to Durango, going through the breathtaking Montezuma Valley's agricultural landscapes.

San Juan Skyway is well-known for its breathtaking natural beauty. Along the trip, you'll pass soaring peaks, craggy mountain ranges, vast valleys, alpine meadows, and crystal-clear rivers. Make sure your camera is prepared so you may record the breathtaking views.

Outdoor Activities: A wide range of outdoor recreational options are accessible from the San Juan Skyway. There are many opportunities to experience the natural beauty of the area, from hiking and mountain biking to fishing, camping, and animal watching.

Historic and cultural landmarks: The byway is a treasure trove of both culture and history. You may tour museums and historical sites, go to ancient mining towns, and discover the region's Native American roots. Spend some time learning about the histories and legacies that formed our area.

food & shopping: There are several food choices available in the villages along the San Juan Skyway, ranging from little cafés to classy restaurants. Additionally, you may visit boutique boutiques, art galleries, and craft shops for one-of-a-kind souvenirs and locally produced things.

Timing and weather: The San Juan Skyway is always open, however the seasons may have a big impact on the weather. Due to snow and ice, winter driving may be difficult, therefore it's wise to check

The Roaring Fork Valley and Aspen

Overview of Aspen

A prominent mountain town called Aspen is located in the center of the Colorado Rockies. Aspen has grown to be a popular destination for tourists from all over the world because to its magnificent natural beauty, world-class skiing, active arts scene, and opulent facilities. An overview of this fascinating town is provided below:

Location: About 200 miles (322 kilometers) southwest of Denver, in Pitkin County, Colorado, is Aspen. It is surrounded by the breathtaking peaks of the Elk Mountains and is located at a height of 8,000 feet (2,438 meters).

History and heritage: During the silver boom of the late 19th century, Aspen was first established as a mining community. The many aspen trees that cover the nearby mountain slopes are the source of the town's name. While the mining sector finally went out of business, Aspen had a resurgence in the middle of the 20th century as it developed into a premier ski resort and cultural center.

Winter sports and skiing: Aspen is known for its world-class snowboarding and skiing. Four top-notch ski resorts can be found in the town: Aspen Mountain, Aspen Highlands, Buttermilk, and Snowmass. Visitors may enjoy a range of slopes appropriate for all ability levels on more than 5,500 acres (2,225 hectares) of skiable terrain in total. The community also provides options for winter hiking, snowshoeing, and cross-country skiing.

Summer Activities: Aspen is a popular summer vacation destination in addition to the winter months. In the middle of breathtaking alpine vistas, outdoor enthusiasts may partake in pursuits like hiking, mountain biking, fly fishing, whitewater rafting, and golf. There are stunning hiking routes and natural splendor at the neighboring Maroon Bells, two recognizable peaks that are sometimes considered to as the most photographed mountains in North America.

Cultural and Arts Scene: Aspen is home to a bustling cultural and arts scene that draws well-known musicians, performers, and artists. Every year from late June to early August, the Aspen Music Festival and School hosts a series of concerts and shows featuring top artists. The Aspen Institute, a well-known think tank and educational institution that sponsors talks and activities on a variety of subjects, is also located in the town.

Shopping and Dining: While exploring the quaint streets lined with Victorian-era buildings, visitors can browse high-end fashion, jewelry, and home decor at Aspen's many upscale boutiques, art galleries, and designer stores, particularly along its famous downtown area known as "Aspen's Luxury Row." The town is renowned for its outstanding eating options, which include award-winning restaurants and a range of cuisines, from gourmet food to regional delicacies inspired by the mountains.

Events & Festivals: Aspen conducts a number of events and festivals all through the year to highlight its rich cultural offerings. These include the

Wintersköl Celebration, a winter-themed event with parades, fireworks, and outdoor activities, the Aspen Ideas event, the Aspen Film Festival, the Aspen Food & Wine Classic, and the Aspen Ideas Festival.

Preservation of Natural Beauty: Aspen takes great pleasure in its dedication to environmental preservation. To safeguard its natural surroundings and preserve its beauty for future generations, the municipality has put in place sustainable practices and preservation initiatives.

Aspen is a tempting destination for all sorts of tourists because of its distinctive blend of natural beauty, outdoor activity, cultural depth, and upscale facilities. Aspen is certain to create a lasting impression, whether you're looking for heart-pounding activities on the slopes, immersing yourself in the arts and culture, or just enjoying the town's opulent amenities.

Snowboarding and skiing

In Aspen, Colorado, skiing and snowboarding are the most popular winter sports. Aspen provides an unmatched experience for both novice and experienced skiers because to its world-class resorts, copious snowfall, and varied terrain. What you need know about skiing and snowboarding in Aspen is as follows:

Aspen is home to four world-class ski resorts, each with its own distinct personality and amenities:
Aspen Mountain, commonly known as Ajax, is a resort with difficult terrain for experienced skiers and riders that is situated in the center of Aspen. It offers an amazing experience for anyone

wanting a daring adventure, with steep courses, glades, and moguls.

Aspen Highlands: Popular with advanced and elite skiers, Aspen Highlands is known for its difficult terrain. It includes the fabled Highland Bowl, where skiers may experience breath-taking backcountry terrain.

Buttermilk: Known for its mellow slopes and pleasant ambience, Buttermilk is ideal for novices and families. With plenty of terrain suitable for beginners and top-notch ski schools, it is the perfect resort for learning to ski or snowboard.

The biggest ski area in Aspen, Snowmass has plenty to offer everyone. It has a broad variety of terrain, including open groomers, wooded glades, and difficult steeps. Additionally, Snowmass has a premier terrain park and a specialized learning area.

Skiable terrain covers more than 5,500 acres (2,225 hectares) among the ski resorts in Aspen. There are slopes appropriate for skiers of all abilities, from groomed lines for novices to difficult bowls and chutes for specialists. For the best conditions throughout the season, the resorts offer modern snowmaking equipment, well-kept trails, and plenty of snowfall.

Lessons in skiing and snowboarding are available for all ages and skill levels at Aspen's ski resorts, whether you're a beginner or an experienced skier wishing to improve your technique. Skiers of all levels may get individualized tuition from qualified instructors who can help newcomers feel at ease on the slopes and improve their abilities.

Lift Systems and Access: Skiers and snowboarders are quickly and effectively transported up the mountains by the resorts in Aspen's lift systems. Time spent on the slopes is increased by easy access to different resort areas provided by high-speed chairlifts and gondolas.

Terrain Parks: Aspen's resorts provide outstanding terrain parks for skiers looking for an adrenaline rush and a chance to show off their abilities. A variety of jumps, rails, and other elements appropriate for freestyle skiing and snowboarding are included in these parks.

Backcountry and Cat .Skiing: Backcountry skiing and snowboarding are also possible in the mountains that surround Aspen. Skiers with experience may use snowcats to visit pristine backcountry regions for exploration while being guided by experts, or they can choose to go cat skiing.

After a day of skiing or snowboarding, Aspen has a thriving après-ski culture. At slopeside pubs and lounges, you may relax and mingle while taking pleasure in live music, cool drinks, and delectable snacks. Aspen also offers a variety of eating establishments, from fast food joints to fine dining establishments, where you can indulge in après-ski meals and sample a variety of cuisines.

Rental stores in Aspen provide a wide selection of high-quality pieces of equipment if you don't already have your own ski or snowboard equipment. To meet your tastes and experience level, these businesses provide a large assortment of skis, snowboards, boots, and helmets.

Aspen offers an unparalleled skiing and snowboarding experience thanks to its famous resorts, diverse terrain, and breathtaking mountain panoramas. Aspen's slopes are likely to wow this winter, whether you're an expert looking for a demanding adventure or a novice taking your first ski lesson.

Summertime Excursions and Outdoor Activities

Even while Aspen is known for its world-class winter sports, there are plenty of outdoor activities and experiences to enjoy throughout the summer. Here are some summertime activities and outdoor leisure choices in Aspen, from hiking and mountain biking to river rafting and paragliding:

Hiking: All ability levels may enjoy the network of beautiful hiking trails that encircle Aspen. Discover the Maroon Bells-Snowmass Wilderness, home to renowned walks including the Crater Lake Trail and the Maroon Lake Scenic Trail. Stunning panoramas and animal interactions may also be found on the Hunter Creek Trail, Smuggler Mountain Trail, and Cathedral Lake Trail, which are all well-liked choices.

Mountain biking: Aspen has a robust trail network that attracts fans of the sport. There is something for every biker, from difficult singletrack tracks to easy concrete roads. Hire a bike and ride the thrilling Government Trail, the picturesque Rio Grande Trail, or the downhill slopes and attractions of the Snowmass Bike Park.

Fly fishing: The rivers and streams around Aspen provide excellent possibilities for fly fishing. Cast your line into one of the trout-rich Crystal River, Fryingpan River, or Roaring Fork River. There are guided fly fishing excursions available to assist you in navigating the waterways and developing your abilities, regardless of your level of experience.

Experience the exhilaration of whitewater rafting or kayaking on the raging rivers close to Aspen. Take a guided rafting excursion down the Roaring Fork River's difficult rapids or take a leisurely float down the quieter portions. There are also thrilling whitewater rafting opportunities on the adjacent Arkansas River.

Take to the sky and take in a fresh view of Aspen's breathtaking scenery with paragliding and hot air ballooning. Try paragliding to feel free and fly over the mountains while catching thermals. Alternatives include taking a hot air balloon flight and seeing the expansive vistas of the nearby summits.

Riding a horse: Set off on a pleasant equestrian excursion through Aspen's beautiful surroundings. You may go through highland meadows, deep woods, and along raging rivers on guided trail rides. Discover the wilderness while getting in touch with nature and the spirit of the Old West.

Rock Climbing: Rock climbers of all skill levels may enjoy the rocky landscape in Aspen. You may try your climbing prowess on the granite cliffs and crags in the region, which offer everything from easy climbs to difficult ascents. There are guided climbing expeditions offered for individuals who want training and safety direction.

Play a game of championship golf while taking in the mesmerizing mountain vistas at Aspen's golf courses. With beautiful mountain scenery as its background, the Aspen Golf Club and Snowmass Club Golf Course provide difficult fairways and well maintained greens.

Camping and hiking: Adventures in camping and backpacking are possible in Aspen's wilderness regions. Set up camp in authorized areas or go on multi-day hiking expeditions across the Hunter-Fryingpan or Maroon Bells-Snowmass Wildernesses.

Outdoor Events and Festivals: Aspen holds a number of outdoor events and festivals that honor music, the arts, culture, and outdoor pursuits throughout the summer. A few of the yearly highlights are the Aspen Ideas Festival, Aspen Music Festival and School, Aspen Food & Wine Classic, and JAS Aspen Snowmass Music Festival.

The summer season in Aspen provides a variety of activities to suit every interest and ability level, whether you're looking for heart-pounding thrills or tranquil outdoor pleasures. Enjoy exhilarating outdoor activities while taking in the natural splendor of the Rockies.

Indoor Activities

The town of Aspen provides a range of indoor activities for individuals looking for entertainment, leisure, or cultural experiences even though it is well renowned for its breathtaking outdoor adventures. The following are some indoor pastimes you may enjoy in Aspen:

Art Galleries: Aspen is home to a large number of galleries that display a wide variety of artwork, including modern and contemporary works as well as Native American and Western pieces. Take in the thriving art scene by exploring the galleries in Aspen's downtown.

Museums & Cultural Centers: Explore the Wheeler/Stallard Museum to discover Aspen's history and traditions, or go to the Aspen work Museum to see exhibits of thought-provoking modern work. Additionally, a number of locations are run by the Aspen Historical Society, including the Holden/Marolt Mining & Ranching Museum and the Wheeler Opera House.

retail: The upmarket retail environment in Aspen is well-known. Explore the designer shops, upscale boutiques, and specialty stores that line the streets of downtown Aspen. These establishments sell apparel, jewelry, accessories, and home goods.

Spa and wellness: Visit one of Aspen's top-notch spas to indulge in some pampering and relaxation. Spend some money on a massage, facial, or body treatment for yourself, or indulge in restorative activities like hot springs, saunas, and steam rooms. Yoga and meditation programs are provided by several spas in Aspen to promote further health and relaxation.

Dining & Culinary Experiences: Aspen's dining scene consists of more than just its top-notch eateries. To learn new methods and dishes, take into consideration attending a cooking class or taking part in a culinary workshop. These opportunities often involve the opportunity to learn from master chefs in-person and the chance to sample your own creations.

Catch a musical or performance at the Wheeler Opera House, which presents a range of concerts, plays, movies, and comedic performances. World-class artists play classical music throughout the summer at the Aspen Music Festival and School.

At the Aspen Center for Environmental Studies, you may interact with Aspen's natural environment via educational events and displays. With the help of interactive exhibits and guided tours, discover more about the local ecosystem, animals, and conservation initiatives.

Breweries and Wine Tastings: There are several wine stores and tasting rooms in Aspen where you may taste a variety of wines from across the globe. Alternately, go to one of Aspen's breweries to sample locally produced beer and see how it is made.

Visit the Aspen Recreation facility (ARC), which has a number of amenities, including swimming pools, ice rinks, a climbing wall, and a fitness facility, to stay active inside. Tennis, bowling, and even indoor golf simulators are some indoor sports that you may enjoy.

Film screenings and festivals: The historic Wheeler Opera House offers a variety of indie, vintage, and international film selections all year long. Aspen also holds the Aspen Film

Festival, which features a broad range of movies and documentaries.

The town's thriving arts, history, and culinary sectors are easily accessible via Aspen's indoor activities, whether you're looking for cultural enrichment, leisure, or amusement. You may still have a meaningful and fun day exploring the interior attractions of this intriguing mountain town even when the weather is not conducive to outside pursuits.

A Natural Wonder, Maroon Bells

One of the most magnificent natural marvels in the United States is commonly acknowledged to be Maroon Bells, which is situated nearby Aspen, Colorado. Maroon Bells provides a genuinely breathtaking experience with its imposing peaks, pure alpine lakes, and bright autumn colors. What you need know about this amazing place is as follows:

Maroon Peak and North Maroon Peak are two imposing summits that make up the Maroon Bells in the Elk Mountains. Over 14,000 feet (4,267 meters) high, these peaks, sometimes known as the "Maroon Bells," rise abruptly from the surrounding terrain. The mountains' steep, symmetrical sides, which are made of sedimentary mudstone, give them a unique and arresting aspect.

Maroon Lake is a magnificent alpine lake that reflects the surrounding wildness and high hills. It is located at the foot of the Maroon Bells. A photographer's fantasy scenario is created by the picture-perfect combination of the surrounding aspen forests' vivid colors and the crystal-clear waterways.

Outdoor pursuits: Maroon Bells is a paradise for nature lovers. Visitors may take advantage of hiking routes that lead to panoramic views throughout the summer at places like Crater Lake, where they can get a close-up look at the Maroon Bells. For more seasoned hikers, the Maroon-Snowmass Trail and West Maroon Pass are popular choices. The region is a popular spot for leaf-peeping in the autumn as the aspen trees change from green to various colours of gold and orange.

Viewing Wildlife: A variety of animals, including deer, elk, bighorn sheep, and even the rare black bear or mountain lion, may be seen in Maroon Bells. While exploring the region, nature lovers may keep an eye out for these amazing species, but it's crucial to remain a safe distance from wildlife and preserve its ecosystem.

Opportunities for photography: For good reason, Maroon Bells is often cited as one of the most popular destinations in the United States. Photographers have many opportunity to capture the magnificence of the Maroon Bells reflected in Maroon Lake or framed by the surrounding nature thanks to the breathtaking sceneries, particularly at dawn and dusk.

Accessibility: From downtown Aspen, it is a picturesque 9-mile (14.5-kilometer) journey to the Maroon Bells. A shuttle service is offered in the summer and autumn to lessen traffic and save the fragile habitat. It's important to keep in mind that entry for private cars to Maroon Bells is limited at busy times, so you should arrange your trip accordingly.

Visitor Center and Interpretive Programs: The Maroon Bells Visitor Center offers details on the geology, vegetation, and animals of the region, as well as its history. Park rangers are on hand to respond to inquiries and provide knowledge about the area's natural beauties. The facility also provides informative lectures and led treks that deepen awareness of the Maroon Bells' ecology and cultural importance.

Leave No Trace: When visiting Maroon Bells, like in any natural environment, it's crucial to follow Leave No Trace guidelines. To conserve the area's natural beauty for future generations, this entails respecting the environment, remaining on approved paths, properly disposing of garbage, and having as little influence as possible.

A trip to Maroon Bells is sure to be an experience you won't soon forget, whether you're a nature lover, photographer, or just looking for some peace and quiet. It is a must-visit location for anybody traveling the Aspen region due to the magnificence of the peaks, the serenity of Maroon Lake, and the surrounding nature.

Festivals, the Arts, and Culture

Aspen, Colorado, is well-known for its outdoor recreation opportunities and scenic surroundings, as well as for its thriving arts, culture, and festival scene. Here is a sample of the creative and cultural offerings that contribute to Aspen's success as a cultural center:

Aspen Art Museum: The Aspen Art Museum is a famous museum of modern and contemporary art. It hosts a variety of changing exhibits that highlight cutting-edge contemporary art. Through its thought-provoking exhibits, seminars, and educational events, it seeks to excite and challenge visitors.

Theatre Aspen: Theatre Aspen is a reputable theater group that puts on a range of live productions, such as musicals, plays from the past and the present, and plays for young audiences. The Hurst Theatre, tucked away in Rio Grande Park, hosts top-notch shows all summer long.

The Aspen Music event and School is a well-known summer music event that draws excellent talent from all around the world. Enjoy superb classical music performances by famous players and gifted students, ranging from symphonic concerts to chamber music recitals.

The Anderson Ranch Arts Center is a premier facility for the study of the visual arts, including classes, talks, and exhibits. It gives artists and art aficionados a place to explore a range of creative mediums, such as painting, sculpture, ceramics, photography, and printing.

The Aspen Santa Fe Ballet is a highly regarded modern dance group that puts forth original and enthralling performances. Watch how their gifted dancers use expressive gestures and innovative choreography to bring tales to life.

Festivals & Events: Aspen holds a wide variety of festivals and events all year long that highlight the town's broad cultural heritage. Influential intellectuals, decision-makers, and artists come together at the Aspen Ideas Festival for stimulating talks. A selection of top-notch musical acts are presented at the JAS Aspen Snowmass Music Festival in a breathtaking outdoor environment. The Aspen Film Festival, Aspen Laugh Festival, and Aspen Words Literary Festival are further noteworthy occasions.

Visit the venues of the Aspen Historical Society, such as the Wheeler/Stallard Museum and the Holden/Marolt Mining & Ranching Museum, to fully immerse yourself in Aspen's rich past. The interesting displays, artifacts, and guided tours offered by these museums explore Aspen's mining, ranching, and cultural legacy.

The Aspen Institute is a worldwide think tank and educational institution that encourages discussion and interaction on significant global topics. Numerous events are held there, including as conferences, seminars, and lectures by well-known philosophers, decision-makers, and artists.

Art Galleries: Aspen has a thriving art culture, with several galleries displaying a variety of creative styles and materials. Discover the creations of local, American, and worldwide artists by perusing the galleries in Aspen's downtown.

Aspen Film: Aspen Film is a nonprofit organization whose mission is to advance and present the cinematic arts. They provide a platform for both known and up-and-coming filmmakers by hosting a range of film screenings, such as independent films, documentaries, and special events.

Aspen has a diverse cultural environment that appeals to art aficionados, music lovers, and those looking for intellectual stimulation, from visual arts to performing arts. Explore the galleries, watch performances, and take part in the many festivals and events that Aspen hosts all year long to fully experience the city's creative energy.

Learning about the Western Slope

Grand Junction and the National Monument in Colorado

Grand Junction, a picturesque community in western Colorado, provides a starting point for exploring the area's breathtaking natural settings, which include the Colorado National Monument. The Colorado National Monument and Grand Junction are described in the following manner:

Grand Junction: Grand Junction is the biggest city in western Colorado and a regional center for the arts, culture, and outdoor recreation. A variety of stores, eateries, art galleries, and historic buildings make up the downtown district, which has a lively and pleasant vibe.

Colorado National Monument: The Colorado National Monument, which is located just outside of Grand Junction, is a spectacular natural marvel distinguished by red rock canyons, soaring monoliths, and expansive views. The 20,000-acre monument provides a variety of outdoor pursuits and picturesque driving.

Scenic Drives: The major route that travels through the Colorado National Monument, the Rim Rock Drive, provides breath-taking vistas at every bend. This 37-kilometer (23-mile) beautiful route follows the cliffs and offers multiple pullouts for picture-taking and quick walks.

paths & Hiking: The Colorado National Monument is home to a network of paths for hikers of all experience levels. Popular treks include the Devil's Kitchen Trail, which leads to an unusual rock structure, and the Serpents Trail, a historic path that ascends the canyon cliffs. One of the most prominent sights in the park, the Independence Monument, is reached through the Monument Canyon Trail.

Rock climbing: The Colorado National Monument draws rock climbers from all over the globe with its rocky cliffs and difficult terrain. While novice climbers may enjoy guided climbing experiences appropriate for all abilities, experienced climbers can take on the vertical cliffs and challenging routes.

Bighorn sheep, mule deer, coyotes, and several bird species are among the animals that may be seen at the Colorado National Monument. As you wander the park, keep an eye out for these majestic animals because you could be rewarded with glimpses of them in the wild.

Opportunities for Photography: The Colorado National Monument's striking red rock formations, narrow valleys, and vast views provide photographers several chances to take beautiful pictures. The landscape is given a magical quality by the interaction of light and shadow during dawn and dusk.

The Colorado National Monument Visitor Center offers displays, information, and ranger-led programs that provide insights into the park's geology, wildlife, and cultural history. It's a terrific place to start your tour. Deepen your understanding of the natural marvels of the monument by learning about the distinctive geological processes that formed it.

Picnicking and camping: The Saddlehorn Campground, located within the Colorado National Monument, offers a tranquil picnicking and camping experience. Take in the tranquility of the park, enjoy a picnic among breathtaking views, and spend the night under a sky full of stars.

Cycling and mountain biking: Mountain bikers and road cyclists alike love to visit the Colorado National Monument. Exhilarating rides across the park's breathtaking sceneries are made possible by the difficult terrain and picturesque pathways.

Grand Junction and the Colorado National Monument provide an unforgettable experience, whether you're looking for stunning vistas, outdoor pursuits, or a peaceful retreat into nature. Discover the fascinating rock formations, take in the splendor of the canyons, and take part in the variety of outdoor activities that make this area a must-see location for nature enthusiasts.

Tastings & Vineyards in Wine Country

Colorado may not be the first place that springs to mind when thinking of wine, but the state is home to a growing wine industry, and Grand Junction serves as the entrance to Colorado's wine region. An overview to the local wineries and taster events is provided below:

The biggest and most well-known wine area in Colorado is the Grand Valley American Viticultural Area (AVA), which lies close to Grand Junction. The AVA benefits from its distinctive microclimate, which has warm days and chilly nights and offers ideal growing conditions for grapes.

The Grand Valley AVA is home to several wineries and vineyards that produce a variety of wine varieties and styles. Two Rivers Winery, Colterris Winery, Carlson Vineyards, and Red Fox

Cellars are a few well-known wineries. Each vineyard provides tastings, tours, and the opportunity to learn about the winemaking process. Each winery also has its own distinctive personality.

Wine tastings: A lot of the local vineyards feature tasting rooms where guests may try a range of wines made there. Red, white, and rosé wines are often included at tastings so that guests may experience the distinctive tastes and qualities of Colorado wines. There is often knowledgeable personnel on hand to answer inquiries and provide insights into the wines.

Vineyard Tours: Some wineries have guided vineyard tours that let customers explore the scenic orchards, discover the many grape types cultivated nearby, and learn about the viticultural techniques used in the making of Colorado wine.

Wine Festivals and Events: Throughout the year, Grand Junction and the surrounding region hold a number of wine festivals and events that provide visitors the chance to experience a variety of Colorado wines in one place. One of the biggest and most well-known wine festivals in the state is the Colorado Mountain Winefest, which takes place each year in Palisade (a hamlet close to Grand Junction).

Wine and Food Pairings: Many wineries in the Grand Valley AVA also provide guests with the opportunity to partake in a food matching experience, which allows them to sample wines with locally produced cheeses, charcuterie, or gourmet foods. These pairings improve the tasting experience by emphasizing the ways in which different tastes enhance and compliment the wine.

Wine Education: Some local wineries and wine stores provide educational programs, courses, and seminars for individuals looking to delve further into the world of wine. These programs provide wine lovers the chance to broaden their horizons, develop their wine appreciation skills, and discover the subtleties of Colorado wines.

Wine Trails: The Grand Valley Wine Trail links many of the local vineyards and is a well-known circuit. Visitors may experience the variety of Colorado's wine offerings by following the path as they conveniently and picturesquely tour many vineyards.

Grand Junction and the adjacent wine region provide a pleasant experience for wine enthusiasts, from sipping on award-winning wines to meandering through scenic vineyards. A trip to the vineyards and wineries in this area gives you the opportunity to sample the distinctive tastes of Colorado's expanding wine industry, whether you're an expert or a casual lover.

National Park of the Black Canyon of the Gunnison

In western Colorado, there lies a magnificent natural marvel called Black Canyon of the Gunnison National Park. An overview of this gorgeous location is provided below:

Geological Wonder: The Gunnison River's erosive action over millions of years eroded the Black Canyon of the Gunnison, creating its stunning and sheer cliffs. The deep, tight canyon is a geologist's paradise with its steep walls, dim shadows, and unusual rock formations.

beautiful Drives: The park provides a number of beautiful drives with breath-taking canyon vistas. Both the South Rim Road and the North Rim Road lead travelers around the canyon's rim, providing breathtaking vistas and chances to take in the rough beauty and sheer plunge of the canyon walls.

routes for Hiking: There are several hiking routes in Black Canyon of the Gunnison National Park that are appropriate for hikers of all levels of experience. Hikers may explore the varied terrain and get up close to the stunning vistas by taking anything from leisurely strolls around the rim to strenuous descents down the canyon. The Oak Flat Loop, Warner Point Nature Trail, and the difficult but worthwhile Inner Canyon paths are a few well-liked trails.

Viewing animals: A wide variety of animals, including mule deer, elk, bighorn sheep, and other bird species, may be seen in the park. While exploring the canyon, keep your eyes peeled because you could come upon one of these gorgeous animals in its natural setting.

Photography options: The Black Canyon of the Gunnison provides many options for photography aficionados with its spectacular rock formations, imposing cliffs, and constantly shifting light. Document the complex patterns on the canyon walls, the play of light and shadow, and the size of the terrain.

Rock climbing: Rock climbers from all over the globe come to the Black Canyon to scale its craggy rocks. The park has difficult climbing routes, both for conventional and sport climbing. In order to climb in the Black Canyon, one needs expertise, experience, and the right safety gear.

Opportunities for fishing and river sports are provided by the Gunnison

River, which cut the canyon. While kayakers and rafters brave the treacherous rapids that run downstream from the canyon, anglers may try their luck capturing trout in the river's clear waters.

Ranger-led activities are available throughout the park, and they include stargazing events, campfire discussions, and guided walks. The knowledge and respect of visitors for this special location is increased through these programs, which provide insights into the ecological and cultural history of the canyon.

Wilderness Camping: For those looking for a more immersive experience, Black Canyon of the Gunnison National Park provides wilderness camping options. Permits are available for backpackers who want to enter the designated wilderness areas, where they may spend the night beneath the stars and awaken to the peace of the canyon.

Viewing the Night Sky: The park is a great place to observe the night sky due to its distant position and little light pollution. Visitors may take in the beauty of the night sky by seeing a brilliant display of stars and constellations on clear evenings.

A hidden jewel, Black Canyon of the Gunnison National Park provides hikers, photographers, and outdoor explorers with an untamed and breathtaking experience. Discover the canyon's depths, take in the breathtaking views, and marvel at the geological wonders that make this park one of Colorado's must-see attractions.

Thermal Baths and Relaxation

Many natural hot springs can be found in Colorado, making it the ideal place to unwind and rejuvenate. The state's hot springs and relaxation opportunities are listed below:

Glenwood Hot Springs: One of the world's biggest natural hot springs pools, Glenwood Hot Springs is situated in Glenwood Springs. The hot springs include a large, kid-friendly pool as well as a more intimate, hotter therapeutic pool. While soaking in the warm, mineral-rich waters, guests may take in the scenery of the surrounding mountains.

The rustic and natural atmosphere of Strawberry Park Hot Springs, which is close to Steamboat Springs, is appealing. The hot springs, which are surrounded by woodlands and include a number of pools with varied temperatures, let guests relax in the calming waters. Steam rising from the ponds in the middle of snowy landscapes throughout the winter adds to the setting's allure.

The Mount Princeton Hot Springs Resort is a collection of hot springs pools that is situated in Nathrop, close to Buena Vista. Stunning mountain beauty surrounds the natural hot springs, where visitors may relax. The hotel also has a spa and wellness area where visitors may enjoy calming services like massages and facials.

The exquisite hot springs facility in Ouray, which is also known as the "Switzerland of America," is located there. A variety of pools, including a large lap pool and smaller soaking pools, are available at the Ouray Hot Springs. Visitors may take use of the healing waters while taking in the magnificent views of the mountains around.

Hot Sulphur Springs: This famous hot springs resort has been open for business for more than 150 years and is situated in the town of Hot Sulphur Springs. The facility has a number of pools with various mineral contents and temperatures so that guests may personalize their bathing experience. The calm alpine scenery contributes to the peace and relaxation.

Spa and Wellness Retreats: Colorado is also home to a number of spa and wellness retreats that provide a selection of services for rest and renewal. Natural hot springs are often combined with opulent extras like massages, facials, yoga lessons, and meditation sessions at these retreats. The Springs Resort & Spa in Pagosa Springs and Dunton Hot Springs are two well-liked resorts.

Backcountry Hot Springs: Colorado has backcountry hot springs that may be reached by hiking or backpacking for those looking for a more adventurous experience. These secluded, naturally occurring hot springs often require a moderate to difficult climb to get. They provide a tranquil, remote place for unwinding in the middle of nature.

Colorado's hot springs provide a calming and healing experience, whether you want to visit a developed hot springs resort or explore into the bush. Spend some time relaxing, taking in the scenery, and letting the warm water wash your worry and anxiety away.

Sporting activities and outdoor recreation

Colorado is known for having a sizable outdoor playground that offers a variety of leisure pursuits and adventure sports for both thrill-seekers and nature lovers. Here is a summary of Colorado's outdoor leisure and adventure sport options:

Backpacking and hiking: Colorado has a vast network of hiking routes that range in difficulty from short day hikes to demanding multi-day treks. Discover breathtaking mountain panoramas, alpine lakes, and unique ecosystems by hiking well-known pathways like the Colorado Trail, Continental Divide Trail, or Maroon Bells-Snowmass Wilderness.

Mountain biking: Colorado is a mountain biker's heaven because of its challenging landscape and top-notch tracks. The well-known trails in Fruita and Moab, the difficult descents in Crested Butte, and the exhilarating terrain in Winter Park are all popular vacation spots.

Whitewater Rafting and Kayaking: Colorado's rivers provide exhilarating opportunities for whitewater rafting and kayaking. Adventurers may discover alternatives that are ideal for all skill levels, from the Class II rapids of the Arkansas River to the more difficult Class IV and V rapids of the Clear Creek or the Animas River.

Rock Climbing: Colorado is a sanctuary for rock climbers because to its enormous rock formations and craggy cliffs. For climbers of all skill levels, locations like Eldorado Canyon, Boulder Canyon, and Rocky Mountain National Park provide a range of routes.

Skiing and snowboarding: Colorado is known for its top-notch ski resorts with varied terrain and pristine slopes. Aspen, Vail, Breckenridge, Steamboat Springs, and Telluride are well-known ski resorts with everything from groomed lines to backcountry excursions.

Cross-country skiing and snowshoeing: For those looking for a more sedate winter experience, Colorado's snow-covered landscapes provide fantastic chances for these winter sports. For a peaceful winter trip, check out the routes in places like Leadville, Crested Butte, or Rocky Mountain National Park.

Zip Lining: Take a zip line ride and feel the rush of flying over the trees. Colorado has several places where you may take part in zip line adventures that will give you an adrenaline rush and a unique view of the surroundings.

Take to the sky and enjoy the freedom of paragliding or hang gliding. Beautiful vistas and ideal weather are available in places like Boulder, Golden, and Aspen for these exciting airborne excursions.

Fishing: Colorado is a sanctuary for fishing aficionados because to its magnificent lakes, rivers, and streams. Cast your line into well-known fishing areas to try your luck catching trout or other species, such as the Gold Medal waters of the South Platte River, the Blue River, or the Fryingpan River.

Camping and Backpacking: Colorado has several wilderness campgrounds and backpacking destinations. You may immerse yourself in the grandeur of nature and spend evenings beneath starry sky whether you choose modern campsites with amenities or lonely wilderness camping.

Colorado's outdoor leisure and adventure sports opportunities are endless, from the craggy peaks of the Rocky Mountains to the exciting rivers and gorgeous vistas. Colorado has several possibilities for outdoor enthusiasts to explore and take in the state's charms, whether they're looking for an adrenaline rush or a peaceful retreat into nature.

Mountains and Boulder

Getting to know Boulder's charm

A thriving city snuggled against the Rocky Mountain foothills is Boulder, Colorado. Boulder, known for its breathtaking natural beauty, forward-thinking culture, and vibrant downtown environment, has a special allure that draws tourists from all over the globe. Here is a list of the factors that contribute to Boulder's allure:

A pedestrian-only thoroughfare dotted with shops, galleries, restaurants, and street performers, Pearl thoroughfare Mall is the center of downtown Boulder. Enjoy the bustling atmosphere as you stroll down the brick-paved mall and browse the unique stores and restaurants.

Boulder has a wealth of activities for outdoor leisure, making it a haven for outdoor aficionados. Visit the city's famous Flatirons rock formations on a hike, or explore Chautauqua Park's many miles of trails. At Boulder Creek, you may also go biking, rock climbing, trail running, or swimming.

Chautauqua Park is a historic site and the starting point for breath-taking hiking routes. It is situated at the foot of the Flatirons. Visit the park's theater for cultural events and concerts, go for a leisurely walk, or bring a picnic.

Celestial Seasonings Tea Factory: Take a free tour of the Celestial Seasonings Tea Factory to learn more about the production of tea. Try several teas, including their well-known Sleepytime mix, and peruse the tea store for specialty blends and goods.

University of Colorado Boulder: The campus of the University of Colorado Boulder is a center for scholarly and artistic pursuits. Visit the CU Museum of Natural History, take a stroll across the lovely campus, or see a live performance at one of the university's theater or music facilities.

Boulder Farmers' Market: Don't miss the Boulder Farmers' Market if you're in Boulder during the warmer months. Browse a colorful selection of handcrafted goods, fresh fruit, and regional crafts while taking in live music and the bustling neighborhood environment.

The Boulder Museum of Contemporary Art (BMoCA) is a venue for exhibits of contemporary art that provoke thinking. It is situated in the heart of Boulder. Visit the galleries and become involved in the city's vibrant art scene.

One of the few still operating chautauquas in the United States is the Colorado Chautauqua, which was founded in 1898 and is now a National Historic Landmark. In a stunning mountain environment, this national historic monument provides housing, eating, cultural events, and outdoor activities.

The culinary culture in Boulder is renowned for its vibrancy and emphasis on locally produced, fresh ingredients. Discover a range of cuisines, from farm-to-table restaurants to foreign cuisine, that cater to a variety of tastes and dietary needs.

Progressive principles and sustainability: Boulder takes pride in its dedication to these two ideologies. The neighborhood is renowned for its outdoor lifestyle, active involvement in social concerns, and a strong feeling of community. The city is at the forefront of environmental projects.

The allure of Boulder is found in its breathtaking natural surroundings, lively culture, and distinctive fusion of outdoor activity, intellectual pursuits, and sense of community. Boulder provides an unforgettable experience that embodies the soul of Colorado, whether you want to explore the downtown area, go hiking in the mountains, or immerse yourself in the local culture.

Outdoor Recreation in the Foothills, including Hiking

For those who like the outdoors and the great outdoors, the foothills of Colorado include an abundance of hiking and outdoor activities. The area is ideal for exploration and outdoor leisure due to its visual splendor and closeness to the

Rocky Mountains. Here are a few well-liked recreational pursuits in the foothills:

Eldorado Canyon State Park is a hiking lover's heaven and is situated not far from Boulder. Discover the network of paths that snake through the canyon, providing breath-taking vistas of the South Boulder Creek, picturesque overlooks, and towering cliffs. This park is a popular spot for rock climbing, with a variety of routes appropriate for climbers of all abilities.

Boulder Mountain Parks: Boulder is home to a vast network of open space areas and mountain parks. Popular places to go hiking in Boulder include Chautauqua Park, Sanitas Valley Trail, and Mount Sanitas, all of which provide breathtaking views of the Flatiron Mountains and the city. For a lengthier climb, take the difficult Royal Arch Trail, which offers panoramic views from the summit.

Golden Gate Canyon State Park: Golden Gate Canyon State Park, located west of Golden, has more than 12,000 acres of pure wilderness. A number of hiking routes weave through the park's lush woods, meadows, and picturesque vistas. Other well-liked pastimes in the park include horseback riding, mountain biking, camping, and fishing.

Red Rocks Park and Amphitheatre: Red Rocks Park provides more than simply live music and is famous for its stunning amphitheater. Numerous hiking routes in the park go through unusual rock formations and provide breathtaking views of the Denver cityscape. The Trading Post Trail offers a close-up view of the park's renowned red sandstone formations, so be sure to check it out.

West of Golden, in Clear Creek Canyon, you'll find a beautiful environment for outdoor activities. The canyon is well-known for its cliffs and crags, which are suited for climbers of all skill levels. Along the flowing Clear Creek, there are hiking paths in the region that provide possibilities for picturesque treks and animal viewing.

Staunton State Park is a relatively recent addition to Colorado's state park system and is located southwest of Denver. There are several paths in the park that go through pine woods, meadows, and to beautiful vantage spots. The Staunton Ranch Trail and the Elk Falls Overlook Trail are two well-known walks that both provide stunning natural scenery.

A popular spot for mountain bikers and hikers is Apex Park, which is close to Golden. There is a system of paths in the park that go through pine trees and open meadows. Highlights include the

Enchanted Forest Trail and the Apex Trail, which provide stunning scenery and difficult terrain.

Located close to Morrison, Mount Falcon Park has a variety of simple and intermediate hiking paths appropriate for hikers of all experience levels. The park offers panoramic views of the Front Range and Denver's cityscape, as well as historical ruins like those of the Walker Mansion.

These are just a handful of the many hiking trails and outdoor pursuits that may be found in Colorado's foothills. The foothills provide a wide variety of alternatives to explore and interact with nature, whether you're looking for a strenuous walk, a beautiful stroll, or an adrenaline-pumping experience.

Downtown Boulder and Pearl Street Mall

Boulder's downtown and Pearl Street Mall are both thriving communities that perfectly encapsulate the city's distinct personality. The Pearl Street Mall and downtown Boulder may be seen in the following general order:

The pedestrian-only Pearl Street Mall, located in the center of Boulder, is home to a diverse array of stores, eateries, galleries, street performers, and outdoor cafés. Take a leisurely walk through the bustling environment along the brick-paved mall. I

Shopping: With its wide selection of boutiques, art galleries, specialty shops, and big-name merchants, Pearl Street Mall is a shopper's dream. For one-of-a-kind finds and locally produced goods, peruse independent book stores, clothing boutiques, outdoor equipment stores, and specialty gift shops.

Dining: Take a gourmet journey while exploring the variety of restaurants on Pearl Street Mall. There is food to suit every taste, from sophisticated restaurants to informal cafés serving foreign cuisine and farm-to-table restaurants. Enjoy people-watching as you eat excellent meals while eating al fresco on patios.

Experience Pearl Street Mall's thriving street culture by watching one of the many amazing street performers. The street is alive and vibrant as musicians, jugglers, magicians, and artists perform for onlookers and delight them.

Art & Galleries: The Pearl Street Mall is home to a large number of galleries that feature the creations of regional and local artists. Explore the varied art scene, which includes everything from traditional and Native American artwork to contemporary and modern art. Spend some time appreciating the skill and ingenuity on exhibit in the galleries.

Events & Festivals: Throughout the year, Pearl Street Mall is home to a wide range of festivals and events, providing a window into Boulder's thriving cultural scene. There is always something going on that pulls the neighborhood together, from outdoor concerts and street fairs to art festivals and holiday festivities.

Historic Landmarks: There are a number of historic landmarks in downtown Boulder that give the city beauty and character. Seek out the old Hotel Boulderado, which is renowned for its magnificent Victorian-style design, or the Boulder County Courthouse, a stunning example of classical revival architecture.

Boulder Museum of Contemporary Art: The Boulder Museum of Contemporary Art (BMoCA), which is close to Pearl Street Mall, presents exhibits that provoke reflection on contemporary art in a range of media. To experience the dynamic and always changing world of modern art, visit the museum.

Street Festivals and Performances: Downtown Boulder holds street festivals and performances all year long that engage the local population. There are constantly opportunities to appreciate and celebrate the city's artistic energy, from live music concerts and theatrical shows to the Boulder Creek Festival and the Pearl Street Arts Fest.

Atmosphere & people-watching: One of the delights of going to Pearl Street Mall is just taking in the distinctive ambiance and taking in the different mix of people. Here, the active, progressive community of Boulder comes to life, fostering a welcoming environment.

Boulder's downtown and Pearl Street Mall provide a wonderful selection of eating, entertainment, shopping, and cultural opportunities. You'll be surrounded by Boulder's vibrant and friendly attitude whether you're perusing the stores, eating outside, or watching a performance on the street.

Events and Festivals

The city of Boulder, Colorado, is renowned for having a thriving cultural scene and holds several festivals and events all year long. These celebrations honor the city's rich cultural diversity, music, cuisine, and community spirit. These Boulder celebrations and events are noteworthy:

Boulder International Film Festival: This yearly event features a diverse selection of domestic and foreign movies, including dramas, comedies, and documentaries. Filmmakers, industry experts, and movie buffs from all over the globe attend the festival.

Boulder Creek Festival: This well-liked neighborhood celebration commemorating the start of summer is held during the Memorial Day weekend. Live music, food sellers, art displays, a carnival, and numerous activities along Boulder Creek are all part of the celebration.

Colorado Shakespeare Festival: The Colorado Shakespeare Festival is a must-see event for theater enthusiasts. The festival, which is held in the Mary Rippon Outdoor Theatre on the campus of the University of Colorado Boulder, features a number of Shakespearean plays performed outdoors by skilled actors.

This odd and unusual celebration, called Frozen Dead Guy Days, takes place in Nederland, which is close to Boulder. The most notorious inhabitant of the community, Bredo Morstoel, whose frozen corpse is preserved in a cryonic condition, is the subject of Frozen Dead Guy Days. Live music, coffin races, arctic plunges, and other unusual activities are all part of the festival.

The Boulder Craft Beer Festival, which highlights the finest of Boulder's craft beer culture, will be enjoyed by beer fans. Live music, local brewery sampling, and food vendors are all part of this fun outdoor celebration.

Hanuman event: The Hanuman Festival is a yoga and music event that hosts seminars, courses, and performances over the course of a weekend for yoga students, instructors, and musicians. It gives you the opportunity to develop your yoga practice, meet like-minded people, and encounter yoga's transformational power.

Boulder International Fringe Festival: This interdisciplinary festival of performing arts has a varied schedule of theater, dance, music, and comedy shows. The Boulder International Fringe Festival supports experimental and boundary-pushing acts while giving up-and-coming performers a stage.

Boulder Farmers' Market: Although it is not a typical festival, the Boulder Farmers' Market is a thriving weekly occasion that honors regional agriculture, cuisine, and crafts. During the warmer months, the market is held every Saturday and Wednesday and features a broad range of fresh vegetables, artisanal goods, and handcrafted crafts, as well as live music and a neighborhood vibe.

Downtown Boulder Fall Fest: This yearly event welcomes the changing of the seasons and highlights the finest of Boulder's culinary, musical, and artistic offerings. The Downtown Boulder Fall Fest is a three-day event with live music, beer gardens, a kid's carnival, and an art display.

The Boulder Hometown Festival is a family-friendly event that includes a variety of activities and entertainment. It is held during the Labor Day weekend. Enjoy live music, a 5K run, a carnival, a juried art display, a historic vehicle show, and much more.

These are just a handful of the many festivals and events that are held in Boulder all year long. Boulder has plenty to offer for everyone, offering chances to celebrate, connect, and immerse yourself in the city's dynamic culture, whether you're a lover of movies, music, art, cuisine, or outdoor activities.

Beyond Northern Colorado

Fort Collins: A Characterful College Town

In northern Colorado, there is a thriving and energetic college town called Fort Collins. Fort Collins provides a distinctive fusion of college town vitality and small-town charm. It is well known for its attractive Old Town, outdoor recreational possibilities, and flourishing craft beer culture. Listed below is a summary of what makes Fort Collins unique as a travel destination:

Colorado State institution: Colorado State University (CSU), a famous public research institution, is located in Fort Collins. The presence of the university, which attracts a varied student body and hosts a broad variety of academic and cultural events, adds to the town's lively environment.

Old Town Fort Collins is the city's central business sector and a historic area with well-preserved structures from the late 19th and early 20th centuries. Explore the boutiques, cafés, art galleries, and specialized stores as you stroll through the quaint alleyways lined with brick buildings. Don't forget to see the historic Armstrong Hotel and the quaint small cinema house Lyric Cinema.

Craft beer industry: Fort Collins is sometimes referred to as the "Napa Valley of Beer" because of its strong craft beer industry. Many renowned breweries, like New Belgium Brewing Company and Odell Brewing Co., are located in the city and provide brewery tours and tastings. To try a broad range of locally brewed beers, go on a self-guided brewery tour or sign up for a guided beer tour.

Outdoor activity: Fort Collins is surrounded by stunning natural scenery and provides many options for outdoor activity. Just west of the city, the Horsetooth Mountain Open Space offers hiking, mountain biking, rock climbing, and breathtaking vistas of the Horsetooth Reservoir. Whitewater rafting, fishing, camping, and beautiful drives are available nearby in Poudre Canyon.

Parks and Gardens: Take advantage of the city's parks and well maintained gardens. While the Gardens on Spring Creek provide themed gardens, educational activities, and events, the Annual Flower Trial Garden displays a gorgeous assortment of flowers and plants. City parks like Lee Martinez Park and City Park provide open areas for relaxing, playing sports, and having picnics.

The Fort Collins Museum of Discovery offers fun exhibits and interactive learning opportunities for people of all ages by fusing science, history, and culture. Discover the exhibits on local history, space science, and natural history at the museum, including the well-known "Bison at Horsetooth" exhibit.

Food & Dining: There are many different dining choices in Fort Collins, which boasts a booming culinary culture. There is something for every taste, from farm-to-table restaurants and ethnic diners to food trucks and quaint cafés. Don't pass up the opportunity to taste dishes made with fresh ingredients from nearby farms.

Performing arts and music: Fort Collins has a thriving performing arts and music scene. Attend live performances at places like the Aggie Theatre and the Lincoln Center, where a variety of musical genres are performed by both regional and national performers. Cultural attractions include the OpenStage Theatre & Company and the Fort Collins Symphony Orchestra.

Fort Collins is well known for having bike-friendly infrastructure and culture. It's simple to explore the city on two wheels thanks to the city's wide network of bike lanes and paths. Take a ride on a rented bike along the lovely Poudre River Trail or join in on neighborhood activities like the Tour de Fat cycling parade.

Festivals & Events: Throughout the year, Fort Collins holds a number of festivals and events that draw both residents and tourists. The Taste of Fort Collins,

Bohemian Nights at NewWestFest, and the Colorado Brewers' Festival are just a few of the well-liked yearly occasions that highlight the city's thriving culture, live music, and culinary pleasures.

Fort Collins mixes the charm of a rural town with the young vitality of a college town. Whether you're a traveler

Estes Park in Rocky Mountain National Park

Rocky Mountain National Park in Colorado is a gorgeous location renowned for its imposing mountains, immaculate alpine lakes, and an abundance of animals. Here is a list of the experiences you can have at Estes Park and Rocky Mountain National Park:

Start your excursion at one of the park's visitor facilities, such the Kawuneeche Visitor Center or the Beaver Meadows Visitor Center. You may learn more about the park's trails, animals, and safety precautions here. Exhibits, educational activities, and guided activities conducted by rangers are also available at the visitor centers.

Scenic roads: Rocky Mountain National Park's scenic roads let you take in the natural splendor of the park. With heights exceeding 12,000 feet, the Trail Ridge Road, one of the most spectacular drives in America, provides amazing vistas of the surrounding peaks, valleys, and alpine meadows. An older, unpaved route that offers a more personal and exciting driving experience is the Old Fall River route.

Over 355 miles of hiking paths, from leisurely strolls to strenuous summit treks, may be found throughout the park. The Bear Lake Loop, which provides access to numerous magnificent alpine lakes, and the Emerald Lake Trail, which leads through a gorgeous valley surrounded by high heels, are two well-liked paths. The Alberta Falls Trail, the Dream Lake Trail, and the Sky Pond Trail are a few more noteworthy walks.

Rocky Mountain National Park is home to a wide variety of species. Elk, bighorn sheep, mule deer, moose, and other bird species are to be on the lookout for. You could even see elusive lynx, mountain lions, or black bears. Keep your distance and treat animals with respect as you watch them.

Camping: The park has a number of campsites where you may fully appreciate the surrounds' stunning natural beauty. Campgrounds including Aspenglen, Moraine Park, and Glacier Basin are popular options. It is advised to make reservations, particularly during the busiest summer months. Backcountry camping is an alternative for people looking for a more secluded and intimate experience.

Estes Park: The hamlet of Estes Park serves as the entrance to Rocky Mountain National Park and a wonderful starting point for your explorations. Discover the downtown area, peruse the specialty stores, and savor the regional cuisine. For expansive views of the surrounding mountains, ride the Estes Park Aerial Tramway, or take a leisurely stroll down the Riverwalk to soak in the natural splendor.

Estes Park has a number of events all year long that contribute to the town's energetic environment. There are many chances to explore local culture, music, and cuisine, from the Rooftop Rodeo in

July to the Autumn Gold Festival in September.

Outside of the national park, Estes Park provides a variety of outdoor activities. Enjoy horseback riding through picturesque trails, fly fishing in the Big Thompson River, or renting a bike to explore the town and surroundings. You may also attempt animal trips, breathtaking helicopter flights, and rock climbing.

Rocky Mountain National Park Lodging: If staying in a tent isn't your chosen option, Estes Park and the surrounding area offer a variety of hotel, cabin, and lodge options. Some lodgings have breathtaking mountain views, enabling you to wake up to the park's magnificence.

Photographic Opportunities: Estes Park and Rocky Mountain National Park provide photographers several chances to capture beautiful animals and scenery. Be ready to capture the beauty of nature, whether it's the dawn throwing a golden light on the peaks or a moose grazing beside a serene lake.

Estes Park and Rocky Mountain National Park provide an amazing confluence of

The Agricultural Heritage of Greeley

Greeley, a city in northern Colorado, has a long history of agriculture and is well-known for its ties to the farming and ranching sectors of the economy. Here is a description of the region's experiences and Greeley's agricultural heritage:

Union Colony and Agricultural Roots: Nathan Meeker and the Union Colony established Greeley in 1870 as a planned agricultural town. The village was built with the intention of establishing an idealized agrarian community. Discover the Union Colony's past and the concept of sustainable agricultural methods held by the first inhabitants.

Greeley History Museum: Learn more about the town's agricultural past by visiting the Greeley History Museum. The museum has displays that examine Greeley's history, including its beginnings in agriculture. Explore artifacts, images, and tales that illustrate the evolution of agricultural techniques and the effects of agriculture on the neighborhood.

The Centennial Village Museum, an outdoor museum that highlights the region's agricultural heritage, transports visitors back in time. Explore old structures including a farmhouse, a blacksmith shop, and a one-room schoolhouse. Discover what daily life was like for early settlers and learn about the difficulties and rewards of agricultural life.

Agricultural Festivals: Greeley has a number of festivals and events to honor its agricultural past. One of the country's oldest rodeos is the Greeley Stampede, which takes place every year in June and July. Professional rodeo events, live music, parades, and a carnival are all part of the event. The event honors the ranching and cowboy traditions of the region.

Farm-to-Table Experiences: Greeley and the neighborhood have embraced the farm-to-table trend, providing chances to eat cuisine that is freshly prepared and sourced locally. To experience a variety of seasonal food, handcrafted items, and artisanal goods, visit your neighborhood farmers' market. Additionally, some farms and ranches provide visitors the ability to take agricultural tours and make purchases right there.

Despite not having a direct connection to agriculture, the Colorado Model Railroad Museum in Greeley is nevertheless interesting to visit. The museum exhibits the history of rail transportation, which was crucial to the growth of the agricultural economy, and has a large collection of model trains.

Events and Education in Agriculture: Greeley offers a variety of agricultural events and educational activities all year long. Attend workshops and seminars on sustainable agriculture, animal management, and agricultural methods. Take part in activities that raise public knowledge of agriculture and provide farmers, ranchers, and agricultural enthusiasts the chance to network.

Investigate the agritourism options available in and around Greeley. Visit real farms and ranches to get a close-up look at how agriculture is carried out, to learn about raising crops and managing animals, and to participate in practical activities like harvesting fruit, taking hayrides, or even milking cows. Some farms enable guests to experience the everyday tasks and responsibilities of farming via farm stays.

Colorado State University's Agricultural Research, Development, and Education Center is located in Greeley. Research on a variety of agricultural topics, including as crop productivity, soil health, and water conservation, is done at this site. Investigate the center's displays and instructional offerings to discover cutting-edge agricultural techniques and innovations.

Greeley is a supporter of projects like community gardens and urban farming. Explore neighborhood plots where people gather to develop them and advance sustainable food production. Learn about urban gardening initiatives that produce fruits, vegetables, and herbs on empty lots and other urban areas.

Greeley's agricultural tradition is firmly ingrained in its past and still influences the neighborhood now. You may learn more about the town's agricultural history and the value of farming and ranching by visiting its museums, taking part in agricultural activities, and conversing with local farmers and ranchers.

National Grassland of Pawnee

Northeastern Colorado's Pawnee National Grassland is a distinctive and vast grassland environment that gives visitors an opportunity to experience the beauty and tranquility of the prairie ecology. Here is a description of Pawnee National Grassland and the experiences you may have there:

picturesque drives across grassland: Take picturesque drives through the expansive Pawnee National Grassland. You may enjoy magnificent vistas of the green plains, distant mountains, and rolling hills as you travel along the Pawnee Pioneer Trails Scenic and Historic Byway. Take advantage of the chance to see animals along the journey and the peace and quiet of the vast plains.

Hiking and Nature paths: Visitors may explore the varied ecology on one of the many hiking and nature paths available at Pawnee National Grassland. You may reach the famous Pawnee Buttes, imposing sandstone structures rising from the grassland, by way of the Pawnee Buttes Trail. The Birdwalk route is a brief interpretive route that offers the chance to see native flora and birds.

animal viewing: A wide range of animal species, including pronghorn antelope, deer, coyotes, prairie dogs, and other bird species, call Pawnee National Grassland home. Bring your binoculars and camera so you may see and capture images of the fauna that inhabits the grassland. Remember that animals could be more active in the morning or late in the day.

Birdwatching: Pawnee National Grassland is a sanctuary for birdwatchers because to its varied habitat and clear sky. The grassland is famous for its grassland and prairie bird species, which include ferruginous hawks, mountain plovers, grasshopper sparrows, and burrowing owls. Seek out sites designed for bird watching, and carry a field guide to aid in identifying the many species you come across.

Camping and picnics: For visitors seeking to spend longer time in the region, Pawnee National Grassland provides chances for rustic camping and picnicking. The Crow Valley Campground offers fundamental conveniences like picnic tables and vault toilets while letting guests enjoy the serenity of the grassland beneath a starry night sky.

Finding Hidden Gems in Northern Colorado

Numerous undiscovered attractions in Northern Colorado provide one-of-a-kind and unforgettable experiences. Here are a few things you should look into finding:

The Cache la Poudre River, which is the only "Wild and Scenic" river in Colorado, is known for its stunning splendor and thrilling recreational possibilities. Try your hand at fly fishing for trout, go whitewater rafting or kayaking through the rapids, or just take a tranquil trek along the river's lovely pathways.

Red Feather Lakes is a tranquil and remote location that is tucked away in the foothills to the northwest of Fort Collins. Go paddling, paddleboarding, or fishing while exploring the many lakes. For those looking for a peaceful mountain vacation, the region also has camping, mountain biking, and hiking routes.

The wide area of prairie and grassland known as Soapstone Prairie Natural Area is situated close to the Wyoming border. Numerous animals live there, including raptors, bison, and pronghorn. Discover the hiking routes, go on a trip with a guide to observe the bison herd, or just take in the tranquility and serenity of the grassland.

Virginia Dale is a little historic hamlet on the Colorado–Wyoming border where you may go back in time. Learn about the history of the region and the stagecoach transit period by visiting the Virginia Dale Stage Station, a well-preserved stagecoach stop from the 1860s. The community holds celebrations and festivities to honor its Western background.

Colorado Cherry Company: Visit the Colorado Cherry Company to experience the delectable tastes of Northern Colorado. This family-run enterprise, which is based in Lyons, specializes in everything cherry, from pies and preserves to cherry cider and wine. During the cherry season, indulge in their renowned cherry pies and tour their orchard.

Glen Haven is a lovely and endearing mountain village that is tucked away in the mountains to the west of Loveland. Discover the old General Store, which has served the neighborhood since 1903, and take in the tranquil setting surrounded by nature. There are picturesque roads, fishing holes, and hiking paths in the vicinity.

Visit the Sylvan Dale Guest Ranch, which is close to Loveland, to take in the splendor of a functioning ranch. Take part in ranch activities and educational events, go fishing in the Big Thompson River, or enjoy a horseback ride in the beautiful surroundings. Spend the night in a quiet cabin and experience ranch life in the West.

Greyrock Mountain is a secret treasure just west of Fort Collins for hikers looking for a challenge. The route leads to the peak with sweeping views of the surrounding mountains and plains after passing through a variety of landscapes, including woods, meadows, and rocky outcroppings.

The Great Stupa of Dharmakaya is a revered Buddhist structure and a haven of peace and contemplation that can be found in Red Feather Lakes. Participate in meditation classes, stroll around the lovely grounds, and discover more about Buddhism.

Poudre Canyon lovely Byway: Enjoy a lovely journey through this charming canyon that the Cache la Poudre River carved out. Enjoy the breathtaking views of the river, the high cliffs, and the wooded areas. Take a break at one of the many pullouts and picnic spots to take in the scenery and have a quiet meal in the middle of nature.

The opportunity to escape the masses and learn about the area's natural beauty, history, and distinctive experiences is provided by these hidden jewels in Northern Colorado.

Adventure Activities in Colorado

Kayaking and whitewater rafting

Kayaking and whitewater rafting are exhilarating water activities that let you feel the excitement of negotiating rapids and explore beautiful rivers. Fantastic opportunity exist for both hobbies in northern Colorado. An overview of whitewater kayaking and rafting in the area is provided below:

Rafting in whitewater

Cache la Poudre River: West of Fort Collins, the Cache la Poudre River is one of Colorado's top spots for whitewater rafting. It has parts that are easy for beginners as well as severe Class IV and V rapids. There are guided rafting tours that let you experience the thrill of navigating thrilling rapids while taking in the breathtaking canyon surroundings.

Clear Creek: Another well-liked spot for whitewater rafting is Clear Creek, which is close to Idaho Springs and Golden. From easier Class II and III rapids to more difficult Class IV parts, the river has a range of sections appropriate for various ability levels. Denver is close by, making Clear Creek a practical alternative for both residents and guests.

Kayaking:

Poudre River Park and River Run Park both include kayak-friendly elements including manufactured whitewater rapids, waves, and eddies. Poudre River Park is near Fort Collins, while River Run Park is in the center of downtown

Denver. These parks are ideal for kayakers of all skill levels since they provide a secure setting where they can practice and enjoy themselves on the water.

Upper Colorado River: The Upper Colorado River provides picturesque areas with calm currents that are perfect for recreational kayaking close to Kremmling. Enjoy peaceful river stretches while paddling through lovely valleys and take in the breathtaking mountain scenery.

Lower Blue River: Kayakers may enjoy a mixture of calm water and gentle rapids on the Lower Blue River, which is close to Silverthorne. It's a fantastic alternative for kayakers wishing to discover beautiful river stretches and develop their abilities in a less demanding setting.

Big Thompson River: The Big Thompson River, located close to Estes Park, has a variety of kayaking portions, from placid stretches ideal for novices to parts with Class III rapids for more seasoned kayakers. As you paddle down the canyon and over the rapids, take in the beautiful panorama.

Prior to starting any kayaking or whitewater rafting trip, it's important to It is crucial to put safety first. Always use a personal flotation device (PFD) that fits properly, utilize the right equipment, and if you're new to the activity, think about going on guided excursions or taking lessons. Additionally, keep an eye on the river's flow and ask local guides or authorities if there are any safety warnings or limitations.

Northern Colorado provides exhilarating adventures for water sports fans of all skill levels, whether you decide to go whitewater rafting on the Cache la Poudre River or investigate the kayaking options on the Big Thompson River.

Cycle touring and mountain biking

Cycling and mountain bike lovers will have many chances to enjoy Northern Colorado's beautiful scenery and difficult routes. The area's varied geography, which ranges from hilly regions to rolling hills, provides a variety of possibilities for both road cycling and mountain riding. An overview of cycling and mountain riding in northern Colorado is provided below:

Mt. Bike riding

Horsetooth Mountain Park: This park, which is west of Fort Collins, has a network of mountain bike trails that are appropriate for riders of all ability levels.

Riders may take in picturesque vistas of Horsetooth Reservoir and the surrounding mountains while navigating the system's twists and turns, which range from beginner-friendly routes to more difficult singletracks.

In addition to Horsetooth Mountain Park, Lory State Park also provides chances for mountain riding. There are several different routes in the park, some of which include tricky portions, exhilarating descents, and difficult climbs. The park's many habitats, which include grasslands, woodlands, and rocky terrain, are accessible to riders.

Curt Gowdy State Park is a mountain riding haven that can be found in Wyoming, just north of the Colorado state line. Over 35 miles of well-maintained trails, ranging in complexity from easy routes to challenging singletracks, are available in the park. As you bike, take in the breathtaking backdrop of granite cliff formations, pine woods, and tranquil ponds.

West of Loveland is a place called Devil's Backbone Open Space, which provides a unique mountain riding experience. The trail system offers bikers a difficult and beautiful ride as it goes through beautiful rock formations. While negotiating the trail's challenging portions, take in the expansive vistas of the nearby plains and mountains.

Highway Cycling:

From Estes Park to Black Hawk, the Peak to Peak Highway is a well-known picturesque route that presents difficult road riding. As you travel along this gorgeous path, take in the stunning vistas of the Rocky Mountains, pass through glittering mountain streams, and scale challenging slopes.

Cache la Poudre River Canyon: West of Fort Collins, the Cache la Poudre River Canyon offers a beautiful route for road cycling. Ride beside the river as it cuts through the canyon while being surrounded by dizzying rocks and verdant landscapes. The canyon route has exciting descents as well as strenuous climbs.

Take on Trail Ridge Road in Rocky Mountain National Park for a really spectacular road cycling trip. This route is nearly 12,000 feet above sea level and offers breathtaking views and an amazing riding experience. Be ready for difficult ascents, erratic weather, and stunning vistas of the alpine tundra and mountain peaks.

The gorgeous Red Feather Lakes and Poudre Canyon Loop takes you through the lovely Red Feather Lakes region and beside the Cache la Poudre River in Poudre Canyon. Experience the tranquility of the mountains vistas, ride through the woods, and take in the splendor of the river valley.

While road riding or mountain biking, always put safety first. Wear the proper safety equipment, observe trail etiquette, and pay attention to your surroundings. Additionally, before starting any bike journey, examine the local laws, the state of the trails, and the weather predictions.

Northern Colorado offers a range of paths and routes to accommodate cyclists of all abilities and interests, whether you enjoy the exhilaration of mountain biking or the endurance of road riding. Explore the area's natural splendor on two wheels and take in the beautiful views and exciting thrills.

Bouldering and Rock Climbing

Rock climbers and boulderers will find fascinating chances in Northern Colorado, with a variety of crags, cliffs, and bouldering sites to discover. Whether you're a novice or an expert climber, the area offers appropriate difficulties and stunning views. Here is a description of bouldering and rock climbing in Northern Colorado:

Climbing rocks:

Poudre Canyon: West of Fort Collins, the Poudre Canyon is a well-liked location for rock climbing. Sport climbing, conventional climbing, and multi-pitch climbs are all available in the canyon. The Palace, the Narrows, and the vicinity of Mishawaka are a few famous locations in the canyon.

West of Fort Collins is a reservoir known as Horsetooth Reservoir, which has a number of granite outcroppings that are great for bouldering and sport climbing.

For climbers of all abilities, the Rotary Park region and the Torture Chamber are popular locations.

Big Thompson Canyon: To the south of Estes Park, the Big Thompson Canyon provides fantastic prospects for rock climbing. Climbers may experience the challenge of climbing on quartzite and granite cliffs with a combination of sport climbing and classic routes. The canyon has well-known locales including the Monastery and Combat Rock.

Boulder Canyon: Boulder Canyon, a popular rock climbing location, is located just outside of Boulder. There are several climbing routes available in the canyon, including multi-pitch climbs, conventional routes, and sport climbing. Boulder Canyon is appropriate for climbers of all skill levels because to the variety of rock formations and degree of difficulty.

Bouldering:

The granite rocks around the reservoir may be climbed on in the Horsetooth Mountain Open Space, which is close to Fort Collins. Bouldering aficionados may choose from beginner-friendly to difficult routes in the region.

Rotary Park: A popular bouldering place with plenty of granite boulders, Rotary Park is close to Horsetooth Reservoir. The park is an excellent place to spend a day perfecting your bouldering techniques since it has a variety of difficulties appropriate for climbers of all ability levels.

Carter Lake: West of Loveland, Carter Lake provides bouldering chances along its picturesque coastline. Climbers may enjoy a range of challenges on the granite boulders while taking in the magnificent views of the lake.

Safety is of utmost importance while rock climbing and bouldering, as it is with any outdoor sport. Use the proper safety equipment, just climb to the level of your skills, and be alert of any possible dangers. In order to maintain the climbing regions' natural beauty, it's also crucial to respect the environment and adhere to Leave No Trace guidelines.

Rock climbers and bouldering fans may test their skills and take in the gorgeous surroundings thanks to Northern Colorado's unique rock formations and climbing locations. The area provides an exhilarating and satisfying climbing experience, whether you're ascending granite cliffs in the Poudre Canyon or bouldering on the banks of Horsetooth Reservoir.

Paragliding and hot air ballooning

Hot air ballooning and paragliding are two fascinating choices that let you explore the area's breathtaking landscapes from a fresh perspective if you're looking for a distinctive and thrilling adventure in Northern Colorado. A summary of hot air ballooning and paragliding possibilities in northern Colorado is provided below:

Using a hot air balloon

Estes Park: Depart from Estes Park for a picturesque hot air balloon flight over the towering Rocky Mountains. You'll experience breath-taking vistas of the nearby peaks, valleys, and forests as you fly above the trees. The quiet and unique ride offered by floating in a hot air balloon is calm and peaceful.

Fort Collins: From Fort Collins, ride in a hot air balloon to see the scenic splendor of the city and its surroundings. Enjoy breathtaking views of the Front Range mountains as you float over wide-open spaces, flowing rivers, and lovely farms.

Exploring Boulder by hot air balloon will allow you to take in the Flatirons, Boulder Creek, and the picturesque countryside. As you take in panoramic views of the city's famous monuments and the surrounding natural splendor, softly soar into the air.

Paragliding:

Lookout peak: Located just west of Golden, this peak provides a paragliding launch spot with stunning views of the Front Range mountains and the Denver cityscape. As you soar into the air, collecting updrafts and relishing the freedom of flight, experience the rush of paragliding.

Red Feather Lakes: Red Feather Lakes, which are northwest of Fort Collins, are a well-liked paragliding location.

Paragliders may take off from the undulating hills and wide open areas and fly over the picturesque sceneries.

Boulder Reservoir: In Boulder, there are paragliding options near the Boulder Reservoir. Take off from the approved launch locations, fly over the reservoir, and take in the scenery of the surrounding mountains and the reservoir's beautiful water.

Prior to partaking in hot air ballooning or paragliding, it's crucial to choose recognized, certified operators that place a priority on safety and employ qualified pilots or instructors. They can provide you the tools, directions, and advice you need to guarantee a secure and happy encounter.

Both hot air ballooning and paragliding provide distinctive viewpoints of the breathtaking environment in Northern Colorado, enabling you to take in the area's natural beauties and sceneries from a whole different angle. Whether you decide to glide through the air in a paraglider or softly float in a hot air balloon, these activities guarantee life-changing experiences and great memories.

ATV and Off-Roading Adventures

Off-roading and ATV (All-Terrain Vehicle) excursions provide the ideal chance to explore rocky landscapes and secluded areas for those looking for an exhilarating experience in Northern Colorado. Northern Colorado offers a variety of off-road and ATV excursions, whether you're an adventure seeker or a nature lover. An overview of the area's off-roading and ATV options is provided below:

West of Fort Collins, in the Roosevelt National Forest, are a number of off-roading routes for ATVs and other off-road vehicles. The forest has a variety of topographies, such as thick woods, steep slopes, and picturesque meadows. Thrilling off-road adventures and opportunity to see animals may be had on trails like Old Flowers Road and Pingree Park Road.

Rampart Range Recreation Area: This large network of off-road trails is available to ATV enthusiasts and is located close to Colorado Springs. Riders may enjoy a variety of difficulty levels, from simple scenic routes to more tough and technical terrain, on the more than 100 miles of authorized trails. Beautiful views of Pikes Peak and the other mountains may be had here.

Switzerland route: A former railroad grade that has been transformed into an off-road route, the Switzerland Trail is close to Boulder. This beautiful path offers an exhilarating off-roading experience as it passes through pine woods, wide-open meadows, and rocky terrain. For ATVs and off-road vehicles, the track provides a mixture of simple and challenging portions.

Taylor Park: Located close to Crested Butte in the heart of the Rocky Mountains, Taylor Park has fantastic chances for off-roading and ATV excursions. The region has an extensive system of paths that weave through stunning mountain scenery, alpine meadows, and picturesque valleys. Riders may explore paths with different degrees of difficulty, including high-elevation routes with breathtaking vistas.

It's crucial to adhere to safety precautions and protect the environment while taking part in off-roading or ATV excursions. Always ride on authorized paths, obey posted speed limits and other traffic regulations, and dress protectively, including wearing a helmet. To protect the natural beauty of the places you visit, remember to leave no trace and to be respectful of animals and delicate ecosystems.

All levels of expertise may enjoy exhilarating off-roading and ATV excursions in Northern Colorado's various landscapes and off-road tracks. These heart-pumping activities provide a memorable opportunity to explore the wild beauty of Northern Colorado, whether you decide to go through wooded mountains, overcome rocky terrains, or take in stunning vistas of the area's natural treasures.

Nature viewing and Outdoor Recreation

Trails for Backpacking and Hiking

The abundance of hiking and trekking paths in Northern Colorado provide outdoor enthusiasts the ability to fully appreciate the area's natural splendor. Here are several noteworthy hiking and backpacking paths in Northern Colorado, which range from imposing mountains to tranquil lakes and gushing waterfalls:

Rocky Mountain National Park is a sanctuary for hikers and backpackers, with more than 355 miles of hiking trails. The park provides varied topography and magnificent panoramas, from the well-known paths like the Longs Peak Trail and the Emerald Lake Trail to the more remote ones like the Sky Pond Trail and the Odessa Lake Trail.

The Indian Peaks Wilderness, close to Nederland, has a vast network of hiking trails, including the well-known Continental Divide Trail. Hike to alpine lakes like Blue Lake and Isabelle Lake, or test your mettle on the difficult climb to Pawnee Peak's or South Arapaho Peak's top.

A variety of hiking and trekking opportunities are available in the Cache La Poudre Wilderness, which is located northwest of Fort Collins. You may observe animals and take in breathtaking mountain vistas on trails like the Blue Lake Trail and the Crags Trail, which lead you through deep woods, through clear streams, and into high alpine meadows.

Greyrock Mountain: Greyrock Mountain, which is close to the Poudre Canyon, has a well-traveled hiking track that climbs to a rocky top with expansive views. A moderate to challenging trek, the Greyrock Trail rewards hikers with panoramic views of the neighboring mountains and valleys.

Near Fort Collins, the Horsetooth Falls and Horsetooth Rock trails provide picturesque walks appropriate for hikers of all experience levels. The Horsetooth Rock Trail rewards hikers with breathtaking views of the city and reservoir in exchange for a more strenuous journey to the summit of the rock formation than the Horsetooth Falls Trail does.

Trails weave through beautiful woods, tranquil meadows, and gorgeous valleys in the Diamond Peaks Wilderness, which lies west of Fort Collins. Backpackers often choose the North Diamond Peak Trail and the Lake Agnes Trail for its secluded and tranquil wilderness experiences.

Medicine Bow-Routt National Forest: The Medicine Bow-Routt National Forest in Wyoming, just over the border, has a wealth of hiking and trekking paths. Explore the Snowy Range's breathtaking scenery or go on a strenuous hiking expedition via the Mount Zirkel Wilderness.

Check trail conditions, get any required permits, and bring important gear including adequate footwear, navigational aids, plenty of water, and appropriate clothing layers before organizing a hiking or backpacking trip in Northern Colorado. Additionally, always respect the environment and leave the area as you found it by following the principles of Leave No Trace.

The hiking and backpacking routes in Northern Colorado provide a means to explore the area's natural beauties and go outdoors. You may choose from a variety of paths to suit your interests and skills, whether you're looking for a leisurely stroll to a picturesque lake or an adventurous camping trip in the woods.

RV and camping parks

The abundance of camping and RV park alternatives in Northern Colorado enables tourists to fully appreciate the area's natural beauty and take part in a wide range of outdoor activities. Here are several prominent camping and RV park options in Northern Colorado, ranging from tent camping in scenic locales to RV parks with contemporary amenities:

Rocky Mountain National Park: The park offers a number of campsites with breathtaking views, access to hiking trails, and opportunities to see animals. The three most well-liked campsites in the park are Aspenglen, Moraine Park, and Glacier Basin. Keep in mind that although some campsites accept walk-ins, others need reservations.

West of Fort Collins, in Poudre Canyon, you may camp beside the Cache la Poudre River in a variety of places. With access to fishing, hiking, and beautiful drives, campgrounds including Mountain Park, Kelly Flats, and Jack's Gulch provide alternatives for tent camping and RVs.

Boyd Lake State Park: This park, which is close to Loveland, has a campsite with both tent and RV sites. In addition to hiking and bicycling on surrounding trails, visitors may enjoy boating, fishing, and swimming in the lake.

West of Loveland is Carter Lake, which has a campsite with tent and RV sites that face out over a lovely lake. Camping guests may take advantage of nearby hiking and mountain bike trails as well as water sports, fishing, and stunning vistas.

Located just west of Fort Collins, Horsetooth Reservoir has a number of RV and tent camping facilities. Camping areas around South Bay, Inlet Bay, and Horsetooth Reservoir provide access to hiking trails, picturesque vistas, and water activities like fishing.

A number of tent and RV campsites are available in Golden Gate Canyon State Park, which is close to Golden, Colorado. The park offers a number of beautiful hiking paths, possibilities for fishing, and breathtaking views of the mountains.

State Forest State Park: This campground, which is close to Walden, has a variety of camping choices, such as tent sites, RV sites, and cabins. The park offers chances for hiking, fishing, animal observation, and scenic driving among its beautiful scenery.

Check campsite availability and reservation requirements before setting out on your camping or RV vacation since certain sites may fill up rapidly during busy times. Additionally, become acquainted with the unique features and rules of each campsite or RV park, such as the restrictions regarding pets and quiet times.

Outdoor enthusiasts may immerse themselves in the area's natural beauties and take part in a range of recreational activities at the camping and RV sites in northern Colorado. There are several alternatives available to fit your interests and maximize your outdoor trip, whether you like secluded tent camping or RV camping with contemporary comforts.

Fly fishing and fishing both

There are a ton of places to go fishing in northern Colorado, from vast lakes to tranquil mountain streams. Here are several well-known fishing spots in Northern Colorado for both conventional and fly fishing, suitable for both experienced and novice fishermen:

Cache la Poudre River: The Cache la Poudre River, which flows through the lovely Poudre Canyon, provides fantastic fishing chances. The river, which is well-known for its populations of wild trout, including rainbow, brown, and cutthroat trout, offers anglers both calm sections and more difficult rapids.

Big Thompson River: The Big Thompson River, which flows through the stunning Big Thompson Canyon not far from Estes Park, is well-known for its trout fishing. Anglers may enjoy casting their lines in search of rainbow, brown, and brook trout in parts that are simple to reach.

Numerous alpine lakes and mountain streams rich with trout may be found in Rocky Mountain National Park. For a chance to catch different trout species in a gorgeous mountain backdrop, anglers may check out fishing locations including Dream Lake, Sprague Lake, and Glacier Creek.

Bass, walleye, catfish, and trout are just a few of the species that may be fished for in Horsetooth Reservoir, which lies west of Fort Collins. Anglers may launch their own boats, hire boats, or fish from the beach for an enjoyable fishing day.

Boyd Lake is a well-liked fishing spot close to Loveland with a variety of species, including bass, trout, walleye, and crappie. Shore fishing, boating, and kayak fishing are all possible at the lake.

Near Walden is a lake known for its trophy-sized fish, notably rainbow and brown trout. This lake is known as North Delaney Butte Lake. Fly fishers will have plenty of chances to put their talents to the test and take in the breathtaking mountain landscape that surrounds the lake.

South Platte River: The South Platte River, which is close to the town of Deckers, is a premier fly-fishing location. The river is well-known for its brown and rainbow trout numbers and for its difficult but rewarding fishing conditions. On this beautiful body of water, anglers may practice different fly fishing tactics and put their talents to the test.

Before going fishing in Northern Colorado, be sure you have a current fishing license since there are rules and restrictions. Knowing the local fishing laws, catch limits, and any other limitations put in place to safeguard fish populations and habitats are also crucial.

Anglers of all skill levels may find plenty of fishing options in Northern Colorado's rivers, lakes, and reservoirs. The area's many waterscapes guarantee an enjoyable and memorable fishing experience, whether you like conventional fishing or the fine art of fly fishing.

observing wildlife and watching birds

With its variety of ecosystems that are home to a large number of species, northern Colorado is a refuge for those who like wildlife and birdwatching. Here are some noteworthy spots in Northern Colorado for wildlife viewing and birdwatching, from stately beasts to vibrant bird species:

Rocky Mountain National Park is a top location for wildlife watching because to its diverse habitats and a wealth of animals. Elk, mule deer, bighorn sheep, black bears, and moose should all be seen. Numerous bird species, such as Steller's jays, golden eagles, and white-tailed ptarmigans, call the park home.

The biggest grassland in Colorado, Pawnee National Grassland, provides a rare chance to see prairie animals and grassland birds. While roaming the vast grasslands, keep an eye out for burrowing owls, ferruginous hawks, pronghorn antelope, and prairie dogs.

Jackson County's Walden and North Park provide a variety of habitats for animals. They are both located there. Elk, moose, pronghorn, and coyotes should all be seen. Waterfowl, such as sandhill cranes, great blue herons, and several kinds of ducks, are another attraction in North Park.

Arapaho National Wildlife Refuge: The Arapaho National Wildlife Refuge, which is close to Walden, is a sanctuary for raptors, shorebirds, and waterfowl. Discover the ponds and marshes of the refuge to see wildlife like bald eagles, great horned owls, sandhill cranes, and many waterfowl species.

The Pawnee Buttes, which are in northeastern Colorado, provide a distinctive environment and chances to see prairie species. Hike the paths surrounding the buttes to see prairie falcons, pronghorn, prairie dogs, and other songbirds.

Cache la Poudre River: The Cache la Poudre River offers fantastic chances for birding, particularly during the spring and autumn migratory seasons. Along the riverbanks, keep an eye out for species like belted kingfishers, American dippers, great blue herons, and different warblers.

Barr Lake State Park is a well-known birding location with over 350 species documented. It is located northeast of Denver. To see bald eagles, pelicans, white-faced ibises, and other waterfowl, explore the park's paths and beaches.

Remember to keep a respectful distance from the animals and adhere to any approved paths or viewing places while observing wildlife or birdwatching. To improve your experience and document any sightings, bring binoculars, a field guide, and a camera.

The varied terrain and ecosystems of northern Colorado support a wide variety of animals and bird species. The area provides a wealth of opportunity for unforgettable encounters and the ability to appreciate the beauty of the natural world, whether you are an ardent birdwatcher or just like watching animals in their natural surroundings.

Colorado's Special Places

National Park and Preserve of the Great Sand Dunes

Southern Colorado is home to the extraordinary and stunning Great Sand Dunes National Park and Preserve. The highest sand dunes in North America may be found there, along with a wide variety of other natural marvels and outdoor activities. What to anticipate while visiting Great Sand Dunes National Park and Preserve is outlined below:

The Sand Dunes: The park's greatest draw is its huge sand dunes, the highest of which, Star Dune, rises to a height of more than 750 feet (230 meters). Hikers are encouraged to explore the sand dunes, slide down their slopes on a sled or sandboard, or just take in the surreal surroundings.

Medano Creek: Medano Creek runs along the foot of the sand dunes throughout the spring and early summer, offering a distinctive and pleasant experience. Wading in the shallow water, creating sandcastles, or just relaxing on the creek's beach-like sections are all options for visitors.

Great Sand Dunes National Park and Preserve has a number of hiking paths that are suitable for hikers of all experience levels and interests. The Mosca Pass Trail, Dunes Overlook Trail, and Sand Ramp Trail all provide stunning vistas of the park and opportunity to explore the many ecosystems around the dunes.

Backcountry Camping: The park offers backcountry camping in specified places for those looking for a distinctive camping experience. A unique chance to experience the wonder of the night sky and the serenity of the far-off surroundings is camping among the dunes.

Viewing animal: A variety of animal species have adapted to the distinctive desert habitat of the Great Sand Dunes. While touring the park, visitors could come across mule deer, pronghorn antelope, coyotes, kangaroo rats, and many bird species.

The park provides ranger-led lectures and presentations that shed light on the geology, history, and ecology of the sand dunes. Ranger lectures and Interpretive Center. The visitor center and museum in the park provide displays and information to help visitors better comprehend and appreciate the area's natural beauty.

Recreational options are also available close by at the Great Sand Dunes National Park and Preserve. Zapata Falls, a beautiful cascade tucked away in a small canyon, and the San Luis Lakes State Wildlife Area, which provides boating, fishing, and birding, are two nearby attractions.

Bring adequate sun protection, drink, and footwear that is comfortable for walking on the sand while visiting Great Sand Dunes National Park and Preserve. Additionally, since circumstances could change throughout the year, check the park's website for any brief closures or limitations.

A mesmerizing location that displays the unadulterated beauty of nature is the Great Sand Dunes National Park and Preserve. A trip to this extraordinary park will undoubtedly leave you with priceless memories, whether you spend your time exploring the enormous sand dunes, taking a dip in Medano Creek, or getting lost in the surrounding wilderness.

National Park of the Black Canyon of the Gunnison

Western Colorado's Black Canyon of the Gunnison National Park is a breathtaking and dramatic location that exemplifies the strength and beauty of the natural world. The Black Canyon, which the Gunnison River carved over millions of years, is distinguished by its deep, narrow valley and high, towering rocks. An outline of what you may learn when you visit Black Canyon of the Gunnison National Park is provided below:

beautiful Overlooks: Several beautiful overlooks are available in the park, and they give breath-taking views of the Black Canyon. Visitors may take in the sheer, untamed cliffs and the Gunnison River weaving its way through the canyon from vantage points including the South Rim, Painted Wall, and Warner Point.

Rim Rock Nature walk: This straightforward 0.8-kilometer (half-mile) walk on the South Rim provides a chance to discover the park's distinctive flora and animals. Interpretive markers placed throughout the path provide details on the region's geology, flora, and fauna.

The Gunnison Route provides a strenuous journey into the heart of the Black Canyon for experienced hikers and climbers. This unmaintained path offers a breathtaking and up-close view of the canyon's walls, but it also demands technical knowledge and permits.

Scenic Drives: The South Rim Road and the North Rim Road both provide scenic drives that include pull-offs and viewpoints that let tourists see the canyon's majesty from various angles. Visitors have access to the bottom of the canyon through the East Portal Road, where they may explore the river and experience the Gunnison River's strength firsthand.

Observing species: A variety of species may be seen at Black Canyon of the Gunnison National Park. As you explore the park's many ecosystems, keep a look out for mule deer, elk, black bears, golden eagles, peregrine falcons, and numerous small animals and bird species.

Wilderness Camping and Backpacking: Within designated wilderness regions, the park provides options for backcountry camping and backpacking. Camping in the untamed environment offers a unique experience and enables guests to fully appreciate the tranquillity of the canyon.

Joining a program taught by a ranger is a terrific opportunity to learn more about the geology, ecology, and cultural history of the park. Programs provide insightful information and enhance your vacation with activities including seminars, stargazing events, and guided walks.

Be prepared with sturdy shoes, sunscreen, and plenty of water before visiting Black Canyon of the Gunnison National Park since the terrain may be difficult. As circumstances may change, it's also a good idea to check for any road or trail restrictions before your visit.

The Black Canyon of the Gunnison National Park provides a captivating fusion of untamed terrain, breathtaking panoramas, and outdoor adventure options. A trip to this exceptional park will undoubtedly leave you with priceless memories, whether you want to camp in the bush, do a strenuous climb, or admire the canyon from its rim.

Park and the Royal Gorge Bridge

Near Canon City, Colorado, there is a well-known site called the Royal Gorge Bridge and Park. This landmark bridge and park, which span the magnificent Royal Gorge, provide tourists with an exhilarating experience complete with beautiful vistas and interesting activities. What to anticipate while visiting the Royal Gorge Bridge and Park is as follows:

The Royal Gorge Bridge, which until 2001 was the tallest suspension bridge in the world, serves as the park's focal point. You'll be treated to panoramic views of the rough canyon and neighboring mountains as you cross the bridge, dangling high above the Arkansas River.

Take a beautiful trip on the park's aerial gondola for a once-in-a-lifetime view of the Royal Gorge and its breathtaking natural splendor. The gondola provides a smooth and comfortable way to take in the breathtaking scenery below, including the roaring river and towering cliffs.

Exciting Rides and Attractions: The park has a variety of exhilarating rides and attractions for thrill-seekers. The Royal Rush Skycoaster, an exhilarating swing that flings you out over the brink of the canyon, will have your pulse racing with excitement. Along with these attractions, the park offers via ferrata, a high-altitude bungee trampoline, and zip lines for thrill-seeking tourists of all ages.

beautiful Overlooks and routes: To truly appreciate the Royal Gorge's natural magnificence, explore the park's beautiful overlooks and hiking routes. The park has a number of vantage spots from where you may see the craggy beauty of the surrounding environment, the rushing river below, and the sheer cliffs. Hiking routes provide options for easy strolls or strenuous excursions, letting you fully appreciate the park's breathtaking environment.

Visitor Center and Historical Displays: Discover the fascinating geology and history of the Royal Gorge area by stopping by the park's visitor center. The center has displays and exhibits that emphasize the local natural beauty and the building of the famous bridge. Learn more about the human tales that have formed the Royal Gorge, the local animals, and the development of the canyon.

The Royal Gorge Bridge and Park features a range of events and forms of entertainment throughout the year. There is always something occurring to enhance your stay and create a joyful mood, from live music performances to holiday festivities.

Dining and shopping: The park has a number of restaurants where you may eat while admiring the Royal Gorge's natural beauty. Grab a bite to eat at one of the park's eateries or cafés, or browse the souvenir and specialty stores for one-of-a-kind presents.

Remember to check the park's website for operating hours, any special events, or closures before visiting the Royal

Gorge Bridge and Park. Due to the park's height, it is important to wear comfortable walking shoes and to dress accordingly for the weather.

The Royal Gorge Bridge and Park, which combines scenic beauty with exciting activities and informative exhibitions, provides an exhilarating and unique experience. A trip to the Royal Gorge Bridge and Park is guaranteed to provide you with priceless memories, whether you're traversing the suspension bridge, flying through the air on a zip line, or just soaking in the breathtaking vistas.

Bishop Castle

In the San Isabel National Forest, close to Rye, Colorado, sits Bishop Castle, a unique and impressive building. The castle, which was built by one guy, Jim Bishop, over the period of many decades, is a striking example of his tenacity and creative vision. What to anticipate while visiting Bishop Castle is as follows:

Architectural Wonder: Bishop Castle is a remarkable illustration of unorthodox design. The castle is a blend of elaborate masonry, ironwork, and distinctive architectural components, standing over 160 feet (49 meters) tall. The attention to detail and quirky details that decorate the castle's interior and exterior will wow you as you explore it.

Visitors to Bishop Castle have the option of taking self-guided tours and exploring the building at their own time. You are welcome to explore the castle's several floors, stairs, and chambers as it is accessible to the general public. Spend some time admiring the workmanship, finding secret corners, and taking in the aesthetic details.

Bishop Castle has a number of turrets and observation decks, which provide breathtaking views of the woodland and hilly surroundings. Reach the castle's summit for expansive views that extend as far as the eye can see and a distinctive vantage point of the surrounding region.

Jim Bishop's creative vision is seen in every nook and cranny of the castle. The inside and outdoor rooms are decorated with intricate wrought ironwork, hand-carved woodwork details, and one-of-a-kind sculptures. Every aspect of the castle is a work of art, reflecting the artist's passion and commitment, making a visit a visual treat.

Continuous Improvements: Bishop Castle is a project that is always changing, undergoing continuous building. As Jim Bishop continues to develop and improve his invention, you could have the chance to see brand-new additions and alterations. This dynamic feature gives the tale of the castle an extra dimension of mystery and intrigue.

Despite being mostly a self-guided attraction, Bishop Castle offers some basic visitor services. Near the castle, there are restrooms and picnic spots, making it simple to stop for a break and take in the scenery while eating a picnic lunch.

Donations & Support: To pay for the building and upkeep of Bishop Castle, Jim Bishop has depended on donations and support from tourists. To secure the castle's survival and preservation for the enjoyment of future generations, think about making a donation.

It's crucial to remember that Bishop Castle is an autonomous enterprise and is not run or subject to regulation by any governmental body while visiting. When touring the castle, use care since there may be sharp turns, confined spaces, and steep spots.

Bishop Castle is evidence of the strength of one man's dedication and vision. For those looking for an unconventional and inspirational experience in Colorado's untamed terrain, it is a must-visit site because to its distinctive architecture, creative embellishments, and gorgeous setting.

Botanical Gardens of Denver

Denver, Colorado is home to the magnificent and varied Denver Botanic Gardens. The gardens, which cover 24 acres (9.7 hectares) and include a variety of plant species from throughout the globe, provide visitors with a tranquil and all-encompassing experience of nature. What to anticipate while visiting the Denver Botanic Gardens is as follows:

Explore a range of gardens and collections that showcase various plant species and environments. Each section provides a distinctive atmosphere and highlights a particular variety of plants, from the vibrant and aromatic Herb Garden to the serene Japanese Garden. The Romantic Gardens, Rock Alpine Garden, and the Water-Smart Garden are further noteworthy gardens.

Conservatory: Enter the Gates Garden Court, a beautiful glass conservatory that houses a tropical sanctuary. You'll discover a variety of exotic tropical plants inside, including palm trees, orchids, and bromeliads. The conservatory offers year-round getaway to bright blossoms and lush vegetation.

Mordecai Children's Garden: Ideal for families, this attraction gives young guests a hands-on and participatory experience. Children may play and discover in themed areas, take part in educational activities, and interact with nature.

Events and exhibits: Throughout the year, the Denver Botanic Gardens hold a number of events and exhibits. There's always something spectacular going on at the gardens, from summer concerts and outdoor movie screenings to seasonal plant exhibitions and art installations. To find out what activities will take place while you are there, see the schedule.

An extension of the Denver Botanic Gardens, Chatfield Farms is located just outside of Denver and provides more chances for exploring. In addition to a thriving farm and native flora, the wide site has a dedicated dog park and beautiful paths.

Education and seminars: For visitors of all ages, the Denver Botanic Gardens offers a variety of educational programs and seminars. These programs provide chances to broaden your understanding of plants and gardening, from horticulture lessons to botanical art classes.

Dining establishments and gift shops: When you need a break, stop by one of the on-site restaurants for a little lunch or snack. Along with interesting botanical-themed souvenirs, books, and gardening supplies, the gardens also include gift stores where you may take a little bit of the gardens home with you.

Check the Denver Botanic Gardens' website before your visit to learn about any special exhibitions, occasions, or timed entrance restrictions. While exploring the gardens, put on appropriate walking shoes, bring sunscreen and a hat for sun protection, and think about bringing a water bottle to remain hydrated.

Within the busy metropolis of Denver, the Denver Botanic Gardens provide a serene and charming haven. It's a must-visit location for nature lovers, garden aficionados, and anybody looking for a tranquil refuge in the middle of the city thanks to its various plant collections, educational activities, and pleasant outdoor areas.

The Historical Sites of Colorado

Mesa Verde National Park

Southwest Colorado's Mesa Verde National Park is a UNESCO World Heritage site known for its well-preserved ancient cliff dwellings and extensive Native American heritage. Discovering Mesa Verde provides a rare chance to go back in time and take in the amazing architectural and cultural accomplishments of the original Pueblo people. What to anticipate while visiting Mesa Verde National Park is as follows:

Cliff homes: The park is renowned for its magnificent cliff homes, which were built between the sixth and the twelfth centuries by the ancestors of the Pueblo people. These homes had exquisite stone masonry and ornate construction, and they were constructed under overhanging cliffs. For more information on the creation, importance, and history of some of these homes, including Cliff Palace, Balcony House, and Long House, visitors may trek there or join guided tours.

Ranger-led Programs: Participate in ranger-led activities to learn more about the park's natural and cultural history. The region's history, archaeology, and ecology are explored through informative presentations, evening programs, and demonstrations that are presented by rangers in addition to guided tours of the cliff dwellings.

Mesa Verde provides a number of picturesque routes and vistas that give breath-taking panoramic views of the surrounding surroundings. The Mesa Top Loop Road offers panoramic views of the canyons, mesas, and mountains that make up the park's rough topography as well as access to a number of archaeological sites and overlooks.

Chapin Mesa Archaeological Museum: Begin your excursion with the Chapin Mesa Archaeological Museum, where you may explore exhibits, artifacts, and interactive displays to learn about the past and present of the ancient Pueblo people. The museum gives insights into the everyday life of the ancient people and offers important context for the cliff houses.

Trails & Hiking: Mesa Verde offers a selection of hiking routes that let visitors experience the park's many topographies and historical locations. You may get a close-up look at the region's natural beauty and cultural importance whether you select a quick nature route or a strenuous backcountry trip.

Wildlife and Natural Beauty: Mule deer, coyotes, black bears, and a diversity of bird species may all be found at Mesa Verde. As you go around the park, keep an eye out for these creatures. The park is also home to picturesque landscapes including vast mesas, deep canyons, and unusual rock formations, making it a haven for outdoor lovers and nature photographers.

Visitor Center and Amenities: To assist you in planning your trip, the park's visitor center offers useful information, maps, and exhibitions. Additionally, it has a bookshop where you may buy books, souvenirs, and instructional materials about the park. For those who want to stay longer, there are also campgrounds, picnic spots, and a coffee shop.

It's vital to keep in mind that certain cliff houses in Mesa Verde National Park need guided tours or reservations in advance because to their fragile condition. For the most recent details on accessibility, tour availability, and any seasonal closures, it is advised to check the park's website or get in touch with the visitor center.

Mesa Verde National Park provides an enthralling trip into the past that enables guests to interact with the prehistoric Puebloan culture and see its architectural accomplishments up close. For history aficionados, environment lovers, and anybody looking for a rich cultural experience in the American Southwest, Mesa Verde is a must-visit location because of its amazing cliff homes, magnificent vistas, and educational possibilities.

The National Historic Site of Bent's Old Fort

In southeast Colorado, there is an interesting historical site called Bent's Old Fort National Historic Site. It offers an insight into the frontier lifestyle of the early 19th century and the crucial role it played in the cultural and commercial interchange between Native Americans, trappers, merchants, and pioneers. What to anticipate while visiting Bent's Old Fort is as follows:

Historical Significance: Bent's Old Fort began as a trade station on the Santa Fe Trail in 1833. It functioned as a crossroads for commerce between European-American merchants and the Plains Indian tribes as well as a rest stop for tired travelers. Commerce, diplomacy, and cultural interchange in the area were greatly aided by the fort.

Authentic recreation: The fort you see today is a well researched and historically documented recreation of the original adobe fortification. Visitors get an immersive experience that takes them back to the height of the fort's might thanks to the recreation.

Guided Tours: During knowledgeable guides' tours of the fort, guests are given information about the fort's history, architecture, and inhabitants. Learn about the activities that went place within the fort's walls, including everyday life, commerce, and cultural connections. The guides make the history of the fort come to life, enhancing the experience and imparting knowledge.

Living history performances: During your stay, you can have the chance to see these performances. You may get a close-up look at the everyday activities and abilities of the people who lived in the fort thanks to reenactors dressed in historical garb who demonstrate different tasks including cooking, blacksmithing, and trade.

Explore the exhibits and interpretive center, which has educational displays about the Bent's Old Fort's history, culture, and relevance. A fuller comprehension of the fort's function in the Santa Fe Trail commerce and the contacts between many cultural groups is given via interactive exhibits, artifacts, and multimedia presentations.

Natural and Scenic Environment: The fort is surrounded by a beautiful Great Plains environment, with views of the nearby plains and far-off mountains. Enjoy the surrounding scenery by taking a walk around the fort's outer walls. You could even see some animals, such deer, pronghorn antelope, or other kinds of birds.

activities and Programs for Education: Bent's Old Fort provides a variety of activities and programs for education to visitors of all ages. The history, culture, and traditions of the fort and the Santa Fe Trail are explored in further detail via seminars, lectures, demonstrations, and other special events.

For the most up-to-date information on operation times, guided tour schedules, and any special activities or programs taking place while you are there, consult the park's website or get in touch with the visitor center before your trip.

Visitors may take an enthralling trip back in time at Bent's Old Fort National Historic Site, where they can learn about the fascinating history and cross-cultural interactions that occurred along the Santa Fe Trail. For history buffs, families, and anybody interested in the amazing tales of the American frontier, it is a must-visit location because of its accurate reproduction, expert guides, and immersive environment.

Union Station in Denver

Denver Union Station, a prominent meeting spot and historic transit hub, is situated in the heart of Denver, Colorado. The station, which first constructed in 1881, has undergone substantial reconstruction and restoration to transform it into a lively center of activity that combines transit, eating, shopping, and entertainment. What to anticipate while visiting Denver Union Station is as follows:

Marvel at Denver Union Station's beautiful architecture, which combines old-world beauty with cutting-edge conveniences. The station's Beaux-Arts architecture includes sweeping arches, a sophisticated stone façade, and a towering 65-foot clock. As you tour the building's numerous sections, take time to notice the fine workmanship and detailed features.

Transportation Hub: Denver Union Station serves as a transportation hub by offering access to several means of transportation. It functions as a significant train station for Amtrak trains that link Denver to places all throughout the nation. Additionally, the station acts as the main center for local transit, which includes buses, light rail, and free shuttles.

Great Hall: Enter the Denver Union Station's centerpiece, the famous Great Hall. The large hall has inviting sitting places, a lively ambiance, and a grand ceiling with lovely chandeliers. Take a moment to unwind and enjoy the lively gathering area.

Dining and drinking: Denver Union Station offers a range of dining alternatives, from fast food joints to fine dining establishments. Visit one of the numerous cafés to enjoy a cup of coffee, handmade drinks, or delectable cuisine prepared by local chefs. Additionally, the station is well-known for its hopping bars and rooftop patios, which provide a busy evening environment.

Shopping: Look through Denver Union Station's distinctive boutiques and stores. You may discover a range of places to sate your want to buy, from independent book stores and gift shops to local craftsmen and specialized businesses. Find unique mementos, apparel, accessories, and more.

Crawford Hotel: The Crawford Hotel is a posh and venerable lodging choice that is housed within Denver Union Station. The boutique hotel offers tasteful facilities, exquisitely furnished rooms, and convenient access to the station's attractions. You can really savor Denver Union Station's atmosphere if you stay at the Crawford Hotel.

Events and entertainment: Throughout the year, Denver Union Station holds a variety of events and entertainment. There is usually something going on at the station, from live music performances to art exhibits and cultural events. To find out what's going on when you're there, look at the event calendar.

Denver Union Station provides a distinctive and exciting experience, whether you're traveling through as a visitor, meeting friends for dinner, or just taking in the historic architecture. Its unique combination of history, transit, food, shopping, and entertainment makes it a must-see location in Denver and offers both residents and tourists a vibrant and active environment.

Museum at Molly Brown House

In Denver, Colorado, there is a historical site known as the Molly Brown House Museum that provides insight into the life and legacy of Margaret "Molly" Brown. Molly Brown was a significant character in Denver's history and was well-known for her activism, charity, and survivor of the Titanic tragedy.

What to anticipate from a trip to the Molly Brown House Museum is as follows:

Visit the immaculately maintained Victorian house that previously served as Molly Brown and her family's home. The home, which was constructed in the late 19th century, exhibits the period's architectural design and style. Explore the many rooms and take in the ornate woodwork, exquisite furnishings, and vintage accents.

Guided Tours: Skilled docents provide informative guided tours of the home, sharing intriguing details about Molly Brown's life and the historical setting of the period. Learn about her generosity, advocacy for women's rights, and Titanic journey. The tour focuses on the life experiences, accomplishments, and influence of Molly Brown and her family.

displays that are Interactive: The museum has displays that are Interactive that bring Molly Brown's narrative to life. Learn more about her life, travels, and charitable works by perusing exhibits of personal items, pictures, and artifacts. Learn about Denver's political, social, and cultural landscape in the late 19th and early 20th centuries.

Take a walk around the well kept gardens and grounds that surround the Molly Brown House. Enjoy the tranquil outside area, which is adorned with vibrant flowers, rich vegetation, and quiet sitting spots. The gardens provide a peaceful retreat from the busy metropolis.

Special Events and activities: Throughout the year, the Molly Brown House Museum presents a number of special events, activities, and exhibitions. The deeper investigation of

Molly Brown's life, the Titanic, and Denver's past may be provided via these events, which may include lectures, seminars, performances, and themed displays. For the most recent details on forthcoming activities, see the museum's website.

Browse the museum's gift store to discover one-of-a-kind trinkets, books, jewelry, and other relics of Molly Brown and Denver's past. By buying a personal gift to commemorate your visit, you can help the museum.

Opportunities for Education: The Molly Brown House Museum provides materials and educational activities for students and educators. With the help of these activities, visitors of all ages may get a greater appreciation of Molly Brown's historical significance and the social causes she supported.

A opportunity to go back in time and learn about the life of a significant character in Colorado's history is provided by a visit to the Molly Brown House Museum. The museum offers a thorough and engrossing experience that honors Molly Brown's history and her contributions to society via its educational tours, displays, and exciting activities.

Railroad Museum of Colorado

For anyone interested in trains and history, Golden, Colorado's Colorado Railroad Museum is a must-see attraction. The rich heritage and importance of railways in Colorado and the American West are highlighted in this one-of-a-kind museum. What to anticipate when you go to the Colorado Railroad Museum is as follows:

Exploring the museum's vast collection of vintage locomotives, passenger cars, cabooses, and other railroad items will provide you with a wealth of information. Admire the superbly preserved historic trains that reflect many times and modes of rail travel. Steam and diesel locomotives as well as rolling equipment from many eras of railroad history are included in the collection.

The museum's outdoor exhibit area is a railroad enthusiast's dream come true. Take a walk across the vast grounds to see the many railway carriages and pieces of equipment on exhibit. Take a seat in one of the automobiles and visualize yourself driving across the beautiful historical landscapes of Colorado.

Explore the museum's interior displays to learn more in-depth facts about the development of technology and the significance of railways in Colorado and beyond. Learn about the building of rail lines, the difficulties that the first railroad pioneers experienced, and the significant contribution that railways made to the local economy.

Interactive Displays: Participate in the displays that let you experience the sights and sounds of the train via interactive technology. Explore a mock mine tunnel, drive a miniature train, or experiment with switching and signaling devices. Visitors of all ages will enjoy and learn from these interactive exhibitions.

Turntable in Use: Watch the turntable in use as it rotates historical locomotives and carriages for repair and exhibition. You may see the delicate process of moving and arranging the trains thanks to this special feature.

The Colorado Railroad Museum sponsors a number of unique events throughout the year, as well as train rides. These could include of train rides with a theme, holiday events, model train displays, and educational activities. If there are any events that overlap with your visit, check the museum's schedule.

Research Library and Archives: The museum's research library and archives provide a variety of materials for train lovers and scholars. Learn more about the history and growth of railways in Colorado and the West by looking at books, pictures, maps, and other resources.

Gift store: Browse the museum's gift store for a variety of items relating to railroads, including books, clothing, model trains, and one-of-a-kind trinkets. To remember your trip, bring a piece of train history home.

By immersing you in the world of railways and its enormous influence on Colorado's growth, a trip to the Colorado Railroad Museum gives a fascinating look into the past. The museum offers an engaging experience for visitors of all ages, whether they are railway enthusiasts, history buffs, or just interested about the transportation networks that built the American West.

The Craft Beer Scene in Colorado

An Introduction to the Craft Beer Culture in Colorado

Colorado has established a well-deserved reputation as a mecca for fans of craft beer. The state has developed into a refuge for beer enthusiasts and aficionados from all over the globe because to its burgeoning craft beer culture. An overview of Colorado's craft beer scene and what makes it unique may be found here:

Long and Rich Brewing heritage: Colorado has a long and rich brewing heritage that dates back to the mid-1800s Gold Rush. In order to satisfy the thirsty miners and settlers, breweries sprung up in towns and cities all across the state. The thriving craft beer market that exists today has its roots in this history.

Pioneers of Craft Beer: Colorado is home to some of the nation's first craft breweries, which were instrumental in establishing the craft beer movement throughout the country. The craft beer movement was sparked by well-known brewers like New Belgium Brewing Company, which opened in Fort Collins in 1991, and Oskar Blues Brewery, which opened in Lyons in 1997.

Breweries and Microbreweries: Colorado is home to a sizable number of breweries and microbreweries, ranging in size from modest, neighborhood-based companies to well-known, bigger facilities. Breweries abound in Denver alone, garnering it the moniker "the Napa Valley of Beer." A vibrant craft beer sector is also present in other places including Boulder, Fort Collins, Colorado Springs, and Durango.

Beer Style Variety: Craft brewers in Colorado are renowned for their wide selection of beers, which cater to all tastes and preferences. You'll find something to please your palette, whether you like bitter Belgian-style beers, creamy stouts, crisp lagers, or hoppy IPAs. Brewers in Colorado are renowned for their ingenuity and originality, continually pushing the limits of taste and flair.

Ingredients from Local Sources: Many Colorado brewers place a high value on utilizing ingredients from local sources, including hops, barley, fruits, and spices. The focus on sustainable and local sourcing gives the beers a distinctive and genuine quality by tying them to the area's agricultural past.

Beer Festivals and Events: To honor the state's craft beer culture, Colorado holds several beer festivals and events all year long. One of the biggest and most prominent beer festivals in the nation, the Great American Beer Festival in Denver draws beer lovers from all over the world. The Colorado Brewers' Rendezvous, the Winter Craft Beer Festival, and the Collaboration Fest are further noteworthy occasions.

Beer tourism: The craft beer sector in Colorado has grown to be a major appeal. People go from near and far to enjoy the thriving taproom culture, go on brewery tours, and attend tastings. Numerous breweries provide guided tours that give patrons the chance to learn about the brewing process, speak with the brewers, and try a variety of beers.

Colorado's craft beer scene is renowned for its sense of community and cooperative spirit. Brewers often collaborate on special initiatives to produce one-of-a-kind, limited-edition beers. This attitude of cooperation permeates the whole beer scene, promoting a feeling of neighborhood among brewers, beer fans, and people.

For beer lovers and others curious to discover the innovation, passion, and camaraderie that characterize the state's brewing sector, exploring Colorado's craft beer culture is a joyful adventure. Colorado's craft beer scene provides a fascinating and delectable experience for everyone, whether you're an experienced beer enthusiast or a curious beginner.

Colorado's Culinary and Food Experience

Colorado Farm-to-Table Dining

With a focus on locally produced, seasonally appropriate products, Colorado is recognized for its farm-to-table eating scene. Numerous eateries in the region place an emphasis on sustainable methods and collaborations with regional farmers, guaranteeing that customers will enjoy the freshest tastes while assisting the local food industry. Here are a few well-known farm-to-table restaurants in Colorado:

The Kitchen in Boulder is a leader in the farm-to-table movement and has a cuisine that is influenced by regional and seasonal foods. Their sustainable cooking emphasizes the tastes of Colorado's abundant fruits, meats, and dairy products. The Kitchen also encourages participation in the community and agricultural and food-related education.

Black Cat in Boulder: By running its own farm, Black Cat Farm, Black Cat is a farm-to-table restaurant that elevates the idea. For the freshest and tastiest meals, the restaurant buys the bulk of its products directly from the farm. The restaurant even conducts farm dinners and events, and the menu is always changing to match the farm's seasonal offerings.

Denver's Fruition Restaurant focuses on preparing inventive, seasonally appropriate meals using ingredients sourced from nearby farms and suppliers. With a focus on highlighting the greatest tastes of Colorado, the menu combines traditional and modern American cuisine. The restaurant has won several awards for its farm-to-table philosophy.

Meadowlark Farm Dinners - Various locales: Throughout Colorado, Meadowlark Farm Dinners offers a unique eating experience at a number of lovely locales. The evenings include multi-course meals cooked by neighborhood chefs utilizing fresh produce from neighborhood farms. Guests take pleasure in a shared eating experience while taking in the breathtaking scenery of Colorado.

Denver's favorite neighborhood eatery Potager is known for serving food made with organic and locally sourced ingredients. The restaurant's warm and pleasant ambience enhances the whole eating experience, and the menu constantly changes to emphasize the freshest seasonal ingredients. A large wine selection is also available at Potager, with an emphasis on organic and biodynamic beverages.

The Kitchen - Denver: The Kitchen has a second site in Denver that shares Boulder's dedication to farm-to-table eating. The food of the Denver site is influenced by regional products and culinary customs, offering a distinctive dining experience. Additionally, the restaurant sponsors neighborhood activities and promotes local food projects.

Denver's Union Station is home to Mercantile Dining & Provision, a restaurant that highlights the finest farm-to-table food from Colorado. The restaurant has a market with a variety of commodities made in-house, such as artisanal goods, cheeses, and meats. The bakery and coffee counter provide extra treats, and the cuisine emphasizes seasonal ingredients with a modern flair.

These are just a handful of Colorado's outstanding farm-to-table eating alternatives. There are many eateries all around the state that are committed to displaying the fresh, locally produced products of the area, whether you're in Boulder, Denver, or another section of the state. Discovering Colorado's farm-to-table sector offers a chance to support regional farmers and sustainable agriculture in addition to being a gourmet joy.

Denver's Gourmet Communities

Denver, Colorado is a thriving culinary destination with a number of areas that appeal to foodies. These areas provide a wide variety of eating alternatives, including informal cafes, regional food markets, and cutting-edge fine dining facilities. Here are a few Denver neighborhoods with good restaurants:

Lower Downtown, or LoDo, is a vibrant area of Denver that is noted for its lively environment and food options. A variety of hip eateries, rooftop bars, and gastropubs are available, serving a variety of cuisines. LoDo has something for every taste, from seafood restaurants and artisan brewers to farm-to-table restaurants.

RiNo (River North): Known for its thriving art scene and cutting-edge culinary options, RiNo has established itself as Denver's hippest neighborhood. Numerous craft brewers, martini bars, and chef-driven restaurants can be found in the area. In RiNo, there are several dining halls and food trucks that serve a variety of different cuisines and inventive fusion foods.

Highland: Also referred to as LoHi, Highland is a hip area with a bustling food and drink culture. There are a variety of premium restaurants, family-friendly cafes, and hip pubs in the neighborhood. Highland is renowned for its ethnic food, specialty cocktail bars, and farm-to-table establishments.

Capitol Hill: Capitol Hill is a diversified community with a strong cultural background and a wide variety of eating establishments. You may discover a variety of different cuisines here, such as Middle Eastern, Mexican, Vietnamese, Ethiopian, and Vietnamese, as well as vegan and vegetarian-friendly restaurants. Additionally, the area is home to lively coffee shops, breakfast places, and welcoming local pubs.

South Broadway, popularly referred to as SoBo, is home to a variety of hipster atmospheres and delectable dining options. Numerous ethnic restaurants, including Mexican, Thai, Vietnamese, and Ethiopian ones, can be found in the area. Along with the eateries, there are quaint cafés, small-batch brewers, and specialty dessert establishments.

Cherry Creek: Cherry Creek is a posh area noted for its luxury shopping, but it also has a number of posh restaurants. Contemporary American food, sushi bars, fine dining restaurants, and hip cocktail clubs are all present in the neighborhood. For those wanting an elegant dining experience, Cherry Creek is a terrific choice.

Baker: Baker is a bustling community with a developing culinary scene. A variety of fast food restaurants, coffee shops, and dive pubs may be found here. Craft breweries, hip brunch cafes, and foreign food are all popular in the area. Throughout the summer, Baker also runs a weekly farmers market that features handcrafted goods and local vegetables.

These Denver neighborhoods provide a wide variety of gastronomic experiences that showcase the city's varied food culture. Exploring Denver's gastronomic districts is a wonderful way to sample the culinary options of the city, whether you're looking for premium dining, farm-to-table cuisine, ethnic cuisines, or innovative food and beverage companies.

Food Scene in Colorado Springs

The cuisine scene in Colorado Springs is vibrant and always changing, offering something for every taste and desire. The city provides a wide variety of eating alternatives, using both locally obtained products and cuisines from across the world. Here are some of Colorado Springs's culinary high points:

Downtown Colorado Springs is where you'll find a wide variety of restaurants and diners serving food from many cultures and culinary eras. Farm-to-table restaurants, gastropubs, artisan brewers, and premium eating alternatives are all available. The region is particularly well-known for its thriving food truck industry, which offers a broad variety of cuisines in a relaxed atmosphere.

Old Colorado City: Just west of the city center, this area offers a number of food alternatives as well as a pleasant and historic ambience. A variety of local favorites, specialized stores, cafés, and informal eateries are available in this region. Everything from traditional American food to Italian, Mexican, and other cuisines is available.

Manitou Springs is a quirky town with a range of food options that is located at the foot of Pikes Peak. You may discover a wide variety of tastes to satiate your palate anywhere from quaint cafés and artisanal bakeries to ethnic restaurants and quirky diners.

Ivywild School: Ivywild School is a historically significant structure that has been refurbished to contain a number of restaurants and a brewery. You may find a variety of dining establishments here, including a bakery, coffee shop, cocktail bar, and restaurant offering farm-to-table fare, all under one roof. The distinctive ambience of the building enhances the eating experience.

Area around Broadmoor: The Broadmoor district is well-known for its opulent hotels and fine eating establishments. Many of the area's award-winning restaurants provide a fine dining experience, sometimes with breathtaking vistas. You may savor gastronomic pleasures in this region at anything from classy steakhouses to sophisticated foreign cuisine.

International Cuisine: The varied population of Colorado Springs is mirrored in the city's international cuisine scene. The cuisines available include Thai, Mexican, Indian, Italian, Japanese, Vietnamese, and many more. Food enthusiasts may sample various tastes and genuine meals from across the globe.

Local breweries and distilleries: The craft beer and spirits sector in Colorado Springs is flourishing. Many regional brewers and distilleries provide tours, samples, and distinctive taste characteristics. You may try a variety of beers, including both conventional and innovative brews, as well as artisan spirits prepared using ingredients acquired locally.

The culinary landscape in Colorado Springs is always expanding and changing, with a constant influx of new and innovative projects. The city provides a wide variety of eating experiences to satisfy any palette, whether you're looking for local and sustainable food, foreign delicacies, or craft drinks.

Boulder's Sustainable and Organic Cuisine

Boulder, Colorado is well known for its dedication to sustainable and organic cooking. Locally produced foods, ecologically responsible procedures, and farm-to-table eating are all highly valued in the city's culinary sector. The following are some of Boulder's best organic and sustainable food options:

The Kitchen is a well-known Boulder eatery that emphasizes offering fresh, locally produced cuisine. They provide cuisine that is prepared with organic ingredients, meat that is grown responsibly, and seafood that is caught nearby. In order to provide guests with the freshest and best ingredients possible, The Kitchen also gives priority to collaborations with regional farmers and food producers.

Black Cat: This farm-to-table eatery in Boulder pushes the idea of sustainability to new heights. The bulk of the ingredients for their recipes come from Black Cat Farm, an organic farm they own and run. This guarantees that the food is prepared using sustainable methods and is both fresh and tasty.

River and Woods is a restaurant in Boulder that emphasizes regional, sustainable food with a contemporary touch. To develop a cuisine that showcases the finest of Colorado's foods, they collaborate closely with neighborhood farmers, ranchers, and food artisans. Additionally, the restaurant includes a garden where they cultivate the herbs and vegetables that they use in their meals.

Leaf Vegetarian Restaurant: In Boulder, Leaf Vegetarian Restaurant is a must-visit for anyone looking for organic and sustainable vegetarian and vegan cuisine. When feasible, they use organic vegetables and ingredients, and their menu offers imaginative and delectable plant-based cuisine. Leaf is dedicated to sustainability and reducing their negative influence on the environment.

The Boulder Farmers Market is a thriving center for organic and locally grown food. The market, which is held many times each week throughout the growing season, sells a broad range of artisanal goods from nearby farmers and food producers, including fruits, vegetables, meats, and cheeses. It's a terrific location to become involved in local affairs and promote sustainable farming.

Boulder's The Rayback Collective is a unique meeting spot that includes a food truck park, a beer garden, and a communal area. There are many different cuisines to select from because to the food trucks that operate here, which often favor organic and sustainable products. It's a laid-back and fun place to try out various tastes while promoting neighborhood businesses.

These are just a few of the restaurants, cafés, and specialty food shops in Boulder that adhere to organic and sustainable food practices. Visitors may fully experience Boulder's dedication to local, organic, and sustainable food while savoring delectable dishes that are both ecologically responsible and pleasing to the palate.

Local delicacies and Rocky Mountain Cuisine

A distinct culinary style known as "Rocky Mountain cuisine" draws on the tastes and ingredients of the Rocky Mountain area, which includes Colorado. It incorporates items like game meats, wild mushrooms, berries, and herbs, drawing inspiration from the abundant natural resources of the Alps. The following local specialties and meals represent the spirit of Rocky Mountain cuisine:

Bison: A common ingredient in many cuisines, bison is a cornerstone of Rocky Mountain cuisine. This lean and tasty meat is a favorite among meat eaters and is used to make anything from steaks and burgers to stews and sausages.

Colorado Lamb: Due to the vast pastures and cattle that are fed just grass, Colorado is renowned for its premium lamb. A must-try is Colorado lamb that has been roasted or grilled since it has the region's signature soft and delicious characteristics.

Rainbow Trout: Colorado is a top location for trout fishing because to the availability of beautiful mountain streams and lakes. A popular dish in the area, rainbow trout may be pan-seared, grilled, or baked with regional herbs and flavors.

Morel Mushrooms: In the Rocky Mountains, morel mushrooms are a highly appreciated delicacy. These wild mushrooms are often sautéed with butter and herbs, added to sauces and risottos, and have a unique taste and texture.

Huckleberries, chokecherries, and raspberries are just a few of the wild berries that may be found in the Rocky Mountain area. These berries provide foods a sweet and tart flavor by being added to sweets, sauces, and preserves.

Palisade Peaches: The peaches from the Colorado hamlet of Palisade are well-known. These luscious, tasty fruits may be eaten fresh or used in pies, cobblers, and preserves since they grow well in the area's warm environment.

Green chile: A favorite ingredient in Rocky Mountain cooking, green chile gives food a smoky, spicy flavor. This regional speciality is a must-try for spice lovers, whether it's used in a green chile stew, over burritos, or added to sauces.

Colorado Craft Beer: Although not a particular dish, Colorado's craft beer movement is a vital component of the regional culinary tradition. Pale ales, IPAs, stouts, and lagers are just a few of the many beer varieties produced by the state's many craft brewers. It's a great opportunity to get a taste of the Rocky Mountain cuisine to sample some local artisan beer.

Discover the regional specialties and meals that showcase the distinctive tastes and ingredients of Rocky Mountain cuisine when you visit Colorado. You'll come across a multitude of gastronomic delicacies that highlight the region's rich and diversified food culture, including bison, trout, wild mushrooms, and berries.

Colorado's events and festivals

<u>Boulder's Colorado Shakespeare Festival</u>

William Shakespeare's works are honored annually during the Colorado Shakespeare Festival, which takes place in Boulder. One of the oldest and most famous Shakespeare festivals in the country, it was established in 1958. The Colorado Shakespeare Festival's main characteristics and highlights are listed below:

Performances: A number of professional theatrical performances of William Shakespeare's works are included in the festival. Shakespeare's plays are presented on the inside University Theatre stage and the outdoor Mary Rippon Theatre stage each summer by a brilliant group of performers. Shakespeare's ageless narrative and the enchantment of his language may be fully experienced by audiences.

The Colorado Shakespeare Festival's outdoor productions at the famed Mary Rippon Theatre are one of its distinctive features. The University of Colorado Boulder's scenic campus is the setting for the open-air theater, which offers a lovely background for the performances. Audience members may take in the performances outside, among the breathtaking scenery of Colorado.

Shakespeare's plays are presented in a variety of ways throughout the festival, including both well-known classics like "Romeo and Juliet," "Hamlet," and "Macbeth," as well as lesser-known pieces. A variety of comedies, tragedies, and historical plays are included in each season, giving theater lovers a rich and diverse experience.

Programs for Education: The Colorado Shakespeare Festival is dedicated to education and provides a variety of initiatives geared at energizing and motivating students as well as the general public. Pre-show discussions, backstage tours, seminars, and other special events are among the services offered to help people better understand and appreciate Shakespeare's works.

Community Engagement: To promote the arts and provide possibilities for creative expression, the festival works closely with the Boulder community through partnering with area businesses, groups, and artists. Through the power of theater, it acts as a center for culture, generating a feeling of shared experience and community.

Reputable Artists and Directors: The Colorado Shakespeare Festival draws top talent from throughout the nation, including seasoned actors, directors, and designers. Shakespeare's works come to life onstage thanks to the festival's dedication to creative excellence, which guarantees top-notch performances.

Summer Festival Ambiance: Attending the Colorado Shakespeare Festival involves more than simply seeing the plays; it also involves soaking up the vibrant, joyful atmosphere. Pre-show picnics, live music, and other special activities are often included in the festival, which gives theatergoers of all ages a fun and exciting summertime experience.

Shakespeare's works may be seen in a breathtaking outdoor environment at the Colorado Shakespeare Festival in Boulder. This festival is a must-attend event that highlights the ageless beauty and significance of Shakespeare's plays, whether you're a die-hard

Shakespearean or a theater lover seeking a memorable cultural experience.

The Great American Beer Festival in Denver

The Great American Beer Festival (GABF), which takes place every year in Denver, Colorado, is a widely anticipated occasion. One of the biggest beer events in the country, it attracts beer lovers from all over the globe. An summary of the Great American Beer Festival in Denver is provided below:

The GABF is a multi-day festival that offers a broad range of beer-related events. The festival offers participants a full beer experience by including a sizable beer tasting event, informative lectures, beer contests, cuisine pairings, and special activities.

Beer Tasting: The festival's centerpiece is a beer tasting where visitors may taste a wide variety of beers from brewers all across the nation. A broad range of beer genres, including ales, lagers, stouts, IPAs, and more are featured by brewers from all 50 states. It's a wonderful opportunity to discover the many tastes and workmanship of American beer.

Beer contests: One of the most prestigious beer contests in the world is held at the GABF. Breweries submit their beers for evaluation by a group of industry experts, who rate them according to a number of factors, including aroma, appearance, taste, and overall quality. Medals are given out to winners in many categories, which heightens the excitement and recognizes exceptional brewers and beverages.

Education & lectures: Beer specialists, brewers, and business experts will be giving lectures and presentations during the festival. The history and culture of craft beer are among the subjects covered in these sessions, in addition to beer brewing methods and beer varieties. Attendees may learn more and acquire insights into the world of beer directly from the professionals.

Food Pairings: The GABF offers a range of food vendors and food matching experiences to go along with the beer tastings. Local brewers, food trucks, and restaurants provide mouthwatering food choices that go well with various beer varieties, boosting the entire tasting experience and highlighting Denver's diverse culinary scene.

Special Events and Entertainment: The festival offers more than just beer; it also offers live music, shows, and hands-on activities. Guests may take part in beer-related games and activities, see live performances, and mingle with other beer lovers in a fun and dynamic environment.

Brewer's Studio: The festival's unique Brewer's Studio segment is devoted to brewing innovation and experimentation. It showcases rare and limited-edition brews produced by some of the most forward-thinking and inventive brewers. Attendees will get the chance to sample innovative brews and learn about emerging trends in the craft beer sector.

The Great American Beer Festival in Denver is a celebration of American craft beer that brings together beer enthusiasts, brewers, and business people for a fun-filled day out. The GABF provides a thrilling and delectable voyage into the world of American beer, whether you're a seasoned beer aficionado or just inquisitive about the craft beer sector.

Music Festival and School in Aspen

In Aspen, Colorado, there is a renowned summer music festival and school called the Aspen Music Festival and School. It was established in 1949 and is now known across the world as one of the best classical music festivals in America. An overview of the Aspen Music Festival and School is provided below:

Festival concerts: A broad variety of classical music concerts are presented by the festival, comprising famous performers, up-and-coming artists, and great student musicians. The Wheeler Opera House, Harris Concert Hall, and Benedict Music Tent are just a few of the places in Aspen where concerts are held. Opera productions, chamber music recitals, solo recitals, orchestral concerts, and appearances by special guests are all part of the schedule.

Faculty and Artists: The Aspen Music Festival and School draws world-class professors who are accomplished musicians and lecturers in their professions. These professors provide advice, master seminars, and chances for collaboration to the gifted students enrolled in the institution. In order to enhance the musical experience, guest musicians and conductors often participate in the festival.

Student Programs: For aspiring musicians, the Aspen Music Festival and School offers a distinctive study environment. A wide range of seminars and workshops are available, along with individual tuition, coaching in chamber music, orchestra rehearsals, and other activities. Students have the chance to collaborate directly with professors and take part in performances, exhibiting their talents and acquiring priceless experience.

Operatic instruction and performance are the main emphasis of the Aspen Opera Center, a part of the Aspen Music Festival and School. It provides thorough training for singers, conductors, and stage directors, which culminates in fully produced opera performances with both student and professional performers.

Opportunities for Collaboration: The festival fosters an atmosphere where students, professors, and visiting musicians may work together to produce outstanding music. The festival often features chamber music groups, pairings of instrumentalists and singers, and interdisciplinary initiatives that let attendees experience many musical genres and broaden their aesthetic perspectives.

Masterclasses and talks: The Aspen Music Festival and School also presents a number of masterclasses and talks by renowned artists and business leaders in addition to concerts. Students and participants get the opportunity to learn from some of the greatest in the business during these seminars, which provide insightful discussions on musical interpretation, technique, and career development.

Community Engagement: The festival actively participates in the neighborhood, hosting free performances, public rehearsals, and educational events for spectators of all ages. It aims to open up classical music to everyone, promoting a passion of music and raising the subsequent generation of music lovers.

The Aspen Music Festival and School is an exciting and motivating occasion that honors the artistic splendor of classical music. It continues to mold the future of classical music while dazzling audiences with extraordinary musical experiences thanks to its world-class performances, brilliant faculty, and supportive teaching environment.

(Colorado Springs) Colorado Balloon Classic

Sorry for the mistake, but in Colorado Springs there was a celebration named the "Colorado Balloon Classic" as of my knowledge cutoff in September 2021. Please keep in mind that event schedules and details are subject to change, so for the most accurate and up-to-date information, check the most recent reports from reputable sources or the event's official website.

Hot air balloons' beauty and spectacle were shown during the Colorado Balloon Classic, a well-liked yearly event hosted in Colorado Springs. Here is a summary of what happened:

Hot Air Balloon Launches: The daily hot air balloon launches were the Colorado Balloon Classic's major attraction. If the weather permitted, a spectacular and enthralling spectacle for onlookers would be created by multicolored hot air balloons taking to the sky. The launches often take place in the morning when the weather is ideal.

In addition to the launches, the event often included a balloon glow in the evening. The balloons are attached to the ground for this unique occasion and their burners are lit, producing a stunning show of light balloons against the night sky. Attendees will have a fascinating and distinctive experience.

Activities for All Ages in a Family-Friendly Environment: The Colorado Balloon Classic intended to provide a family-friendly environment with a variety of activities for all ages. A fun-filled day is guaranteed for everyone in attendance with these activities, which may include live music performances, food concessions, artisan stalls, kid-friendly activities, and entertainment.

Opportunities for Photos: The occasion provided wonderful chances for photographers to take beautiful pictures of hot air balloons in flight against the background of the Colorado scenery. Visitors were often urged to bring cameras so they could record the vibrant balloons and attractive sceneries.

Community Involvement: To commemorate the pleasure of hot air ballooning, the Colorado Balloon Classic brought together members of the local community, tourists, and balloon enthusiasts. It promoted a feeling of community and gave individuals a forum to interact and express their passion for this distinctive branch of aviation.

Please be aware that the contents of the event may have changed since the information was last updated in September 2021, or that the event may no longer be taking place. For the most recent details on the Colorado Balloon Classic or other related activities in Colorado Springs, it is advised to visit the official website or local event listings.

Colorado where to shop and outdoor equipment

Shops for outdoor equipment and supplies

In Colorado, there are many alternatives for outdoor equipment and gear businesses that may meet a variety of demands and hobbies. Here are a few of

Colorado's well-known retailers of outdoor gear and supplies:

Outdoor retailer REI (Recreational Equipment Inc.) is well-known and has many stores throughout Colorado. A variety of outdoor items are available from them, including clothes, footwear, camping gear, hiking equipment, biking accessories, and more. The high quality merchandise and skilled employees of REI are well regarded.

Sports Authority: Sports Authority is a significant sports goods shop that offers a wide selection of equipment and apparel for the outdoors. They provide a broad variety of goods, such as camping supplies, hiking and backpacking equipment, fishing equipment, bicycling equipment, and sports clothing.

Cabela's: With a site in Lone Tree, Colorado, Cabela's is a well-known outdoor shop. They specialize on gear for camping, fishing, and hunting. A wide range of outdoor equipment is available at Cabela's, including weapons, fishing rods and reels, camping equipment, apparel, and footwear.

Jax Outdoor Gear: Based in Colorado, Jax Outdoor Gear is a state-wide outdoor shop with locations in Lafayette, Fort Collins, and Loveland. They provide a large selection of outdoor supplies and gear for pursuits including camping, hiking, fishing, hunting, and more. Jax also sells apparel, accessories, and shoes.

Wilderness Exchange Unlimited is a speciality outdoor equipment business with a location in Denver. They concentrate on offering inexpensive outdoor lovers' equipment. They provide a variety of goods, such as apparel, hiking gear, climbing gear, and camping gear.

Bent Gate climbing is a Colorado company that sells equipment for climbing and backcountry skiing. It is based in Golden. They sell a variety of outdoor items, such as clothes, avalanche safety gear, ski and snowboarding equipment, and climbing gear.

Neptune Mountaineering: Located in Boulder, Colorado, Neptune Mountaineering is a well-known retailer of mountaineering and outdoor equipment. They provide a wide range of equipment for outdoor sports including climbing, skiing, camping, and others. They also have skilled employees and provide professional guidance.

These are but a few instances of outdoor equipment and gear shops in Colorado. Additionally, you can come across regional specialty shops, smaller merchants, and internet resources that focus on a particular activity or provide unusual gear possibilities. Prior to visiting, make sure to check the locations, opening times, and product selection of certain establishments.

Colorado's Unusual Shopping Experiences

In order to accommodate a wide variety of interests and tastes, Colorado provides a wide selection of distinctive shopping experiences. Here are some unique shopping opportunities in Colorado, whether you're seeking for handmade crafts, goods created nearby, or one-of-a-kind finds:

Denver's art districts include the Art District on Santa Fe and the RiNo (River North) Art District, both of which are thriving communities for the arts. These locations are well-known for their art studios, galleries, and shops selling distinctive jewelry, clothes, home décor, and artwork. You may immerse yourself in the regional art scene while finding one-of-a-kind and imaginative artwork by exploring these neighborhoods.

Colorado Craft brewers: Many Colorado craft brewers sell their own goods, such as branded clothing, glasses, and other products. Breweries and their taprooms provide visitors the chance to experience local craft beer firsthand and pick up one-of-a-kind mementos that capture Colorado's brewing heritage.

Colorado Farmers Markets: Farmers markets are well-liked all around Colorado, particularly in the summer. Local vegetables, artisanal foods, handcrafted crafts, and other items are shown at these markets. Buying fresh, in-season foods and one-of-a-kind handcrafted things there is a terrific way to support regional farmers and craftsmen.

Colorado is peppered with antique and vintage businesses that provide a treasure trove of one-of-a-kind items. You may browse through a selection of old furniture, antiques, clothes, and accessories at antique stores in well-known locations including Denver's Antique Row and Colorado Springs' Old Colorado City.

Outdoor gear consignment stores have emerged in Colorado as a result of the state's active outdoor culture, offering gently used outdoor gear and apparel at steep discounts. These stores provide an inexpensive method to prepare for your outdoor trips while promoting sustainability by reusing equipment.

Native American Art and Jewelry: Several Native American tribes call Colorado home, and the state's galleries and businesses proudly display their creations. To discover genuine jewelry, ceramics, textiles, and other traditional and modern Native American artwork, look for Native American art galleries and stores.

Colorado created Products: Colorado is home to a large number of stores and boutiques that specialize in selling locally created goods. These include artisanal foods, apparel, skincare products, handcrafted crafts, and more. You may discover unique, locally sourced things while supporting regional companies and craftsmen by purchasing products manufactured in Colorado.

These are just a few examples of the distinctive shopping opportunities Colorado has to offer. Every taste and interest may be satisfied in this state, which has everything from farmers markets and art districts to specialized stores and cultural attractions. Before going, always do your homework on the place in question and confirm its hours of operation.

Galleries of art and regional crafts

Colorado has a thriving arts sector, with many local artisan businesses and art galleries spread out over the state. The following Colorado art venues and locations to find regional crafts are noteworthy:

The Denver Art Museum (Denver) is a renowned cultural institution in Colorado that has a sizable collection of artwork from all over the globe. It displays a range of artistic mediums, such as drawings, paintings, sculptures, textiles, photography, and more. Rotating exhibits including regional, foreign, and local artists are also presented at the museum.

The Art District on Santa Fe is a thriving neighborhood of art galleries, studios, and creative spaces that is situated in Denver. It is a center for modern art, displaying a variety of genres and materials. Every month, the area holds a First Friday Art Walk where guests may peruse galleries, interact with artists, and get fully immersed in the neighborhood's artistic community.

The Colorado Springs Fine Arts Center is a multidisciplinary arts organization including a museum, theater, and art school. It is located in Colorado Springs. A wide variety of visual arts, including modern, Native American, and Hispanic art, are on display in the museum. Additionally, it conducts educational activities for people of all ages and sponsors touring exhibits.

Denver's Tennyson Street Cultural District is well-known for its varied collection of art galleries, boutiques, and independent shops. With galleries presenting a range of creative forms, including painting, sculpture, photography, and mixed media, the strip provides a distinctive shopping experience. It's a fantastic location to find up-and-coming local artisans and distinctive crafts.

The Boulder Arts & Crafts Gallery (Boulder) is a cooperative gallery that showcases the creations of more than 150 regional artists and artisans. It displays a broad variety of handcrafted items, such as jewelry, pottery, textiles, glassware, and carpentry. It's a great location to discover distinctive, locally made gifts and artwork.

The Durango Arts Center is a cultural center in Durango that has galleries, workshops, and performance spaces. It presents revolving exhibits of art that showcase the creations of local and international artists. The center promotes a creative atmosphere in the neighborhood by providing art courses, seminars, and community activities.

The Salida Creative District is a designated area in Salida that honors the creative spirit of the community and the arts. It has a large number of art galleries, studios, and craft stores where you can see the creations of regional artists and craftspeople. Visitors may take a tour of the area, interact with the artists, and buy exclusive handcrafted goods.

These are just a few examples of the Colorado art galleries and locations to find regional crafts. The state has a wide variety of creative expressions and a wealth of artistic ability. You may enjoy the originality and skill of Colorado's native artists by perusing these galleries and gift stores.

Local producers and Farmers Markets

Colorado is renowned for its booming agriculture sector and quantity of locally produced, fresh foods. Farmers markets are a great opportunity to support regional farmers and craftspeople while savoring a colorful and varied assortment of produce, meats, dairy products, and other locally produced items. The following Colorado producers and farmers markets are well-liked:

Denver's Union Station Farmers Market is a well-liked meeting place for both residents and tourists. It is situated right in the center of the city. It provides a variety of fresh vegetables, artisanal foods, handcrafted goods, and other things. The market is open on Saturdays from June through August.

One of Colorado's biggest and most well-known farmers markets is the Boulder Farmers Market, which is located in Boulder. Over a hundred merchants selling locally produced vegetables, artisanal foods, baked goods, flowers, and other items are present on Saturdays and Wednesdays. Additionally, the market includes special events and live music.

Colorado Fresh Markets (Multiple Locations): This company runs a number of farmers markets around the state, including the City Park Esplanade Fresh Market, the Stapleton Fresh Market, and the Cherry Creek Fresh Market in Denver. A broad variety of locally produced vegetables is available at these markets, along with specialized foods, baked products, and handcrafted handicrafts.

The Fort Collins Farmers Market is a thriving market that is open on Saturdays during the summer and on Sundays during the autumn. Numerous regional merchants selling fresh vegetables, meats, cheeses, baked goods, and other items are featured there. Live music and kid-friendly activities are also offered during the market.

Western Colorado Farmers Market (Grand Junction): The Grand Junction Western Colorado Farmers Market is a thriving market that highlights the variety of agriculture in the area. It provides a huge selection of fresh produce, meats, artisanal cheeses, honey, and other locally produced goods. Both Thursdays and Saturdays are market days.

Local Farms and Ranches: Colorado is home to a large number of small farms and ranches that sell their goods directly to customers. You may buy a portion of the food grown on many of these farms at farm stands or via community-supported agriculture (CSA) programs. You may interact with the farmers face-to-face and get more knowledge about the food you eat by visiting these farms.

Specialty Food Producers: Colorado is renowned for its artisanal and distinctive specialty food producers. There are many of small-batch manufacturers in the state, making anything from handcrafted chocolates and freshly roasted coffee to gourmet sauces and preserves. You may find these hidden gastronomic jewels by exploring neighborhood grocers, gourmet markets, and specialized shops.

Bring reusable bags, support sustainable practices, and interact with the sellers at farmers markets and local producers to learn more about their wares and agricultural methods. You may enjoy the distinct tastes of Colorado by embracing its local culinary scene and giving back to the hardworking people who make it all possible.

Gift Shops and Ideas for Souvenirs

There are many alternatives available in Colorado for presents and souvenirs that perfectly depict the state's natural beauty, outdoor lifestyle, and cultural legacy. Here are some suggestions for mementos and places to look for gifts:

T-shirts and Apparel: Look for apparel products like t-shirts, hoodies, caps, and other accessories with Colorado-themed graphics like the state flag, mountains, animals, or well-known locations. Numerous gift stores and outdoor outfitters provide a broad range of clothing with Colorado-inspired designs.

Local Art and Crafts: Look for galleries, art fairs, and shops that feature the creations of regional artists and craftspeople. There are many different types of handcrafted goods available, such as jewelry, ceramics, paintings, photographs, woodwork, and more. These one-of-a-kind items make for memorable and genuine mementos.

Native American artifacts: Native American tribes with extensive cultural traditions may be found in Colorado. Find gift stores that focus on Native American artwork and crafts. Items like homemade jewelry, ceramics, fabrics, dream catchers, and antique instruments could be present.

Local Food Products: Colorado has a thriving food sector, and there are many local food items that are wonderful as presents. To find locally roasted coffee, artisanal chocolates, craft beers, sauces & spices, honey, jams, and other gourmet goodies, look at specialized food stores. These goods are often sold at farmers markets, specialized food stores, and gift shops.

Outdoor Gear and Accessories: If you're traveling to Colorado to partake in outdoor sports, you may want to think about bringing home some outdoor gear and accessories as gifts. Water bottles, camping or hiking gear, backpacks, caps, sunglasses, and trail maps are a few examples of products to look for. These products may be found in abundance at outfitters and retailers that sell outdoor gear.

Postcards and photography: Use photography to capture Colorado's breathtaking splendor. Look for post cards with famous scenery, parks, and destinations. Additionally, you could come across calendars or framed reproductions of the state's breathtaking natural attractions.

Books and Guides: Colorado is home to a variety of natural landscapes and a rich history. Think about investing in books and guides about the state's geology, history, wildlife, hiking routes, and particular locations. These materials may be instructive and inspiring for next explorations.

Investigate neighborhood stores, museum gift shops, visitor centers, and specialist boutiques while looking for mementos and presents in well-known tourist sites. These shops often have a broad variety of Colorado-themed goods to suit a variety of tastes and price ranges. As you gather priceless keepsakes of your stay in Colorado, keep in mind to patronize regional companies and craftsmen.

Must do activities

There are a number of must-do activities in Colorado that give you the chance to fully appreciate the state's scenic beauty, outdoor experiences, and cultural attractions. You should think about include the following activities in your itinerary:

Discover Rocky Mountain National Park's stunning sceneries. You may explore beautiful routes, see animals, and be in awe of the towering mountain peaks there. Be sure to visit well-known locations including Bear Lake, Trail Ridge Road, and the breathtaking alpine panoramas.

Visit Garden of the Gods to take in the striking scenery and unusual rock formations in Colorado Springs. Enjoy the breathtaking vistas while taking a leisurely walk or hiking the trails, all the while learning about the geological history of the region.

Take in the Views from Pikes Peak: Climb Pikes Peak, one of Colorado's most recognizable mountains, to the top.

The panoramic views from the summit are simply breathtaking, whether you choose to drive the picturesque Pikes Peak Highway or go on a more challenging climb.

Discover Mesa Verde National Park: Mesa Verde National Park offers a chance to go back in time as you discover the ancient cliff houses. Learn about the intriguing past and culture of the ancestors of the Pueblo people who once called this site home by taking guided tours.

Enjoy Aspen's Outdoor Adventures: If you're there in the winter, hit the slopes at one of the city's top-notch ski resorts. Enjoy outdoor pursuits in the beautiful nearby mountains throughout the summer, such as hiking, mountain biking, and rafting.

Discover Boulder's Charm: Spend some time there and take in the city's lively, diverse environment. Visit the University of Colorado campus, stroll the Pearl Street Mall, explore the surrounding Flatirons, and experience the farm-to-table food and craft beer culture.

Ride the historic Durango and Silverton Narrow Gauge Railroad for a breathtaking excursion through the San Juan Mountains to experience the thrills of Durango. Explore the quaint downtown area, stop by the neighborhood breweries, and go on outdoor excursions like hiking, bicycling, or river rafting.

Visit the Royal Gorge Bridge: Cross one of the tallest suspension bridges in the world and enjoy the stunning views of the untamed Royal Gorge while you do so. Try the Royal Gorge Zip Line or the Royal Gorge Route Railroad for an adrenaline sensation.

Relax and renew yourself at a natural hot spring in Colorado by taking a soak. Bathing in hot springs is the ideal way to relax, whether you select the renowned hot springs of Glenwood Springs, the serene waters of Pagosa Springs, or the secluded pools in the mountains.

Immerse Yourself in Denver's Culture: Take some time to explore this energetic city and stop by its museums, art galleries, and other cultural landmarks. Discover Denver's vibrant districts including LoDo and RiNo, as well as the Denver Art Museum, Denver Museum of Nature & Science, Denver Botanic Gardens, and more.

These pursuits provide a glimpse of the many adventures Colorado has to offer. Colorado offers a multitude of options to make lifelong experiences, whether you're looking for outdoor activities, cultural discovery, or natural marvels.

Staying Safe

It's critical to place a high priority on your safety and wellbeing when visiting Colorado. Here are some pointers to keep you safe while you're there:

Plan and Prepare: Before beginning any outdoor activity, learn about the region, the state of the path, and the upcoming weather. Make sure you have the right tools, maps, and route information. Learn about the rules and procedures for safety.

Dress Properly: Colorado's weather may be erratic, particularly in the higher areas. Prepare for rapid variations in temperature by dressing in layers. For outdoor activities such as hiking, put on sturdy boots.

Dehydration is a risk in Colorado due to its high elevation and dry environment. Bring water with you and drink lots of it, particularly while exercising. Limit your alcohol intake since it might make the effects of altitude worse.

Be Aware of the Altitude: Different people might be affected by Colorado's high elevation. Give yourself plenty of time to adjust to the altitude, particularly if you are moving from a lower level. Exercise slowly and pay attention to any altitude sickness symptoms, such as headaches, dizziness, or shortness of breath. If your symptoms become worse, go to a lower elevation.

Bears, mountain lions, and other species are among the rich biodiversity that calls Colorado home. Learn about wildlife safety precautions, such as how to properly store food, how to stay a safe distance from animals, and what to do if you come across wildlife.

Exercise care When Outdoors: Whether hiking, skiing, or engaging in other outdoor activities, exercise care and adhere to safety regulations. Ski within your skill level, stay on approved paths, and be cautious of any dangers. Be mindful of currents and water levels while participating in water-related activities.

Observe the "Leave No Trace" principles: Show respect for and use principles of leaving no trace. Reduce your environmental effect, pack away your waste, and leave the places you visit in the same condition that you found them. Respect wildlife and keep your distance from it.

Keep Up with Weather Conditions, Road Closures, and Any Safety Alerts or Warnings: Stay informed. For the most recent information, check with local authorities, tourist centers, or park rangers. It's also a good idea to let someone know about your trip plans and the time you anticipate returning.

Although Colorado's cities typically have low crime rates, adopt conventional safety measures when in urban areas. Use well-lit, crowded locations, pay attention to your surroundings, safeguard your possessions, particularly at night. Stay away from leaving valuables in your automobile, and lock your lodgings tightly.

Considerations for COVID-19: Keep up with the most recent COVID-19 rules and regulations in Colorado. Pay attention to local health advice, maintain excellent cleanliness, put on masks when necessary, and keep social distance when necessary.

You may have a safe and enjoyable vacation in Colorado by being well-prepared, knowledgeable, and exercising caution. Always put your personal safety first and abide by any special instructions or rules given by regional authorities and outdoor organizations.

Accommodation Options

There are many alternatives available in Colorado for lodging that will accommodate different tastes and price ranges. Here are some common options for lodging in the region:

Hotels and Resorts: Colorado has a variety of hotels and resorts, from five-star properties to more affordable alternatives. There are several hotels in major towns like Denver, Colorado Springs, and Aspen that appeal to various interests. Skiing in the winter and outdoor recreation in the summer are popular in resorts in mountainous regions like Vail, Breckenridge, and Telluride.

Lodges and Cabins: Stay in a lodge or cabin to experience Colorado's rural beauty. These lodgings are often found in picturesque locations, such close to national parks or in mountain communities. Lodges provide a blend of luxury and nature, while cabins offer a quiet and intimate experience.

Consider staying in a bed & breakfast for a more individualized and private experience. Bed and breakfast inns may be found all around Colorado, including in rural regions, mountain communities, and historic neighborhoods. They often provide individualized service, fresh breakfast, and distinctive décor.

Vacation rentals: As a result of the growth of websites like Airbnb and

VRBO, tourists looking for a home-away-from-home experience are increasingly choosing to stay in vacation rentals. Apartments, condominiums, cottages, and even bigger properties appropriate for families or groups may all be found as vacation rentals around Colorado.

Campgrounds and RV parks: Due to Colorado's stunning natural surroundings, many outdoor enthusiasts choose to camp. Tent and RV campsites are available at state, federal, and private campgrounds. With this choice, you may spend time in the great outdoors taking part in activities like astronomy, hiking, and fishing.

Hostels are a terrific choice if you're traveling on a tight budget or want a more sociable setting. Major cities and several mountain communities include hostels that provide shared or private rooms, public kitchens, and common spaces where tourists may meet other people.

Guest Ranches: Staying at a guest ranch will allow you to experience Colorado's cowboy lifestyle. These ranches include lodging, food, and a range of activities including hiking, horseback riding, and fishing. It's a unique method to get fully immersed in Western culture.

When deciding where to stay, take into account aspects including your chosen location, the accessibility of nearby activities and attractions, the facilities provided, and your budget. Booking lodging in advance is advised, particularly during busy times or for events that are well attended.

Cost of travel and ideal times to visit

The cost of travel in Colorado may vary based on a number of variables, including the season, lodging options, activities, and mode of transportation. Peak travel times, such as the winter for skiing or the summer for outdoor experiences, are often more expensive. Budgeting is essential for covering costs such as lodging, food, transportation, activity fees, and any supplemental costs like equipment rentals or park admission fees.

It depends on your interests and the activities you want to participate in when it comes to choosing the ideal time to visit Colorado:

The summer months of June through August are Colorado's busiest travel times, particularly in the state's mountainous regions. Whitewater rafting, mountain biking, and other outdoor pursuits are all suitable in the typically good weather with moderate to warm temperatures. Popular tourist locations may, however, be congested, and costs could be higher.

Fall (September to October): As the leaves change color, Colorado's fall season provides stunning scenery. It's a fantastic season for trekking, beautiful driving, and photography. Although the weather is normally pleasant, higher altitudes may see colder temperatures. In comparison to the summer, the fall is also a less expensive and congested period to travel.

Winter (December to February): Colorado is known for its ski resorts, and winter is the best season for participating in winter activities like skiing and snowboarding. Wintertime activities bring the mountain cities, including Aspen, Vail, and Breckenridge, to life. However, since lodging and equipment rentals are more in demand during the winter, travel may be more costly.

Spring (March to May): Colorado's spring weather may be erratic, with varying temperatures and occasional snowstorms. But it's a more sedate time to go, with fewer tourists and more reasonably priced lodging and activities. Exploring low-elevation locations, relaxing in hot springs, and seeing the blossoming of wildflowers are all wonderful things to do in the spring.

It's crucial to remember that weather patterns might differ throughout the state, particularly because of the different altitudes. In comparison to lower elevation regions like Denver or Colorado Springs, higher altitudes like the Rocky Mountains may have milder temperatures and more precipitation.

Consider going in the off-peak seasons (spring and autumn) to maximize your experience and save expenses. You should also plan ahead by making reservations for lodging and activities and being flexible with your trip dates. Be aware of any seasonal restrictions or restricted access to certain sights as well, especially in hilly locations during the winter.

Family Friendly Lodging

Colorado has a variety of family-friendly lodging options to fit a variety of needs and tastes. Here are some alternatives to think about:

Hotels that cater to families include several in Colorado and include features including on-site dining options, swimming pools, and large guest rooms or suites. Additionally, some hotels provide unique activities or programs for kids. Family-friendly hotel rates might change based on the area, features, and time of year.

Renting a vacation home or condo may be a terrific choice for families since it gives them extra room and the convenience of a kitchen that is fully furnished. Through websites like Airbnb or VRBO, you may find vacation homes in many different areas of Colorado. The size, location, and amenities of the rental property will affect prices.

Colorado is home to a large number of resorts that appeal to families and provide activities and facilities that are particularly made for children. These resorts often include kid-friendly amenities including supervised kids' clubs, playgrounds, water features in the pools, and planned family-friendly activities. Depending on the location and degree of luxury, resort prices might vary greatly.

Campgrounds and RV parks: For families, camping may be a fun and cost-effective choice. Numerous campsites and RV parks in Colorado have family-friendly features including playgrounds, hiking trails, and close access to outdoor recreation. Depending on the location and amenities offered, camping and RV park prices vary.

Guest Ranches: Offering horseback riding, outdoor recreation, and a glimpse of Western culture, guest ranches give families a unique experience. There are specific programs and activities for children at several guest ranches. Depending on the location, facilities, and caliber of services offered, guest ranch prices might vary.

It's critical to take the season and demand into account when setting pricing. Prices during peak travel times, such the summer and winter, may be higher than during shoulder or off-peak times. Booking lodgings in advance is recommended, especially for popular family locations or during school holiday times.

Compare costs for several lodging alternatives, make direct reservations with the hotel or via reliable travel services, and be flexible with your vacation dates to discover the best deals. Additionally, keep an eye out for any unique deals or packages that are tailored especially for families or provide reduced prices for kids.

Remember to confirm that the selected lodging has family-friendly features like cribs or rollaway beds, kid-friendly cuisine, and kid-friendly recreational activities.

Family Friendly Activities

Children of all ages may participate in a variety of family-friendly activities in Colorado. Here are a few well-liked choices to think about:

Visit Museums and Scientific Centers: Children may learn via interactive displays at a number of museums and scientific centers in Colorado. The Children's Museum of Denver, the Butterfly Pavilion, and the Denver Museum of Nature & Science are a few of the well-liked options.

Discover State and National Parks: Colorado's state and national parks provide a wealth of options for outdoor exploration and family-friendly activities. Kids may take advantage of hiking routes appropriate for their age, take part in ranger-led activities, see animals, and even try out junior ranger programs.

Experience Theme and Amusement Parks: Colorado is home to a few theme and amusement parks that provide exhilarating rides and family-friendly entertainment. Popular options include Glenwood Caverns Adventure Park in Glenwood Springs and Elitch Gardens in Denver.

Riding picturesque railways: Take a trip on one of Colorado's picturesque railways, such the Cumbres & Toltec Scenic Railroad or the Durango & Silverton Narrow Gauge Railroad. Kids may take in the beautiful scenery and have a special train trip.

Visit Children's Farms and Petting Zoos to Learn About Farm Life: Take the kids to children's farms and petting zoos to engage with friendly animals, feed them, and get knowledge about farm life. For animal interactions, the Denver Zoo and Cheyenne Mountain Zoo are also excellent choices.

Enjoy Water Activities: Kids may have fun swimming, paddleboarding, kayaking, and going down water slides at one of Colorado's many lakes, reservoirs, or water parks. In Denver, Cherry Creek State Park, Chatfield State Park, and Water World are a few of the well-liked locations.

Go on Outdoor Adventures: Take part in kid-friendly outdoor activities like hiking on family-friendly trails, bicycling along gorgeous routes, or having picnics in lovely parks. Family-friendly paths and areas may be found in places like Garden of the Gods and Rocky Mountain National Park.

Attend Family-Friendly Events and Festivals: Throughout the year, Colorado organizes a number of family-friendly events and festivals. For events like parades, live music performances, art workshops, and cultural festivities, check the local event calendar.

Visit Interactive Play Centers: Trampoline parks and indoor play areas provide children with a fun and safe setting in which to burn off energy. Trampolines, climbing walls, arcade games, and other interactive play spaces are often seen at these facilities.

Take a Scenic Drive: Colorado is home to some of the world's most beautiful highways, which provide amazing views of the state's mountains, valleys, and surroundings. Think about planning a road vacation with your family along roads like Rocky Mountain National

Park's Trail Ridge Road or the Peak to Peak Scenic Byway.

When selecting activities for your kids, keep in mind to take into account their age and interests. Additionally, it's a good idea to double-check any required reservations or tickets, age limits, and operation hours.

Street food

The street food culture in Colorado is dynamic and diversified, catering to a range of tastes. Here are some popular alternatives for street food you might consider:

Food trucks, which serve a variety of cuisines, are a popular sight in Colorado's cities and villages. Gourmet burger trucks, taco trucks, BBQ trucks, pizza trucks, Asian fusion trucks, vegan and vegetarian trucks, and many more may be found. There are often organized food truck gatherings and festivals that provide the chance to try a range of foods all in one location.

Farmers Markets: Colorado farmers markets have food booths where you may sample delectable street cuisine in addition to fresh vegetables and locally produced goods. Freshly prepared crepes, gourmet sandwiches, wood-fired pizzas, handcrafted pastries, and other delicious delicacies are available from vendors.

Food Halls: In Colorado, food halls are becoming more and more well-liked since they provide a convenient area where you can discover a variety of food sellers under one roof. These restaurants provide a variety of foods, including gourmet burgers, sushi, poke bowls, salads, and other dishes with foreign characteristics.

Ethnic Street Food: Street food from several cuisines may be found in Colorado, a state with a diversified international culinary scene. There is food to please every pallet, including Mexican street tacos and tamales, Vietnamese banh mi sandwiches, Middle Eastern falafel and shawarma, Indian samosas, and Thai street noodles.

Festivals & Events: Throughout the year, Colorado is home to a large number of street food festivals and events. Food vendors are often present at these events, giving a variety of selections including regional specialties, foreign cuisine, sweet delicacies, and ice-cold drinks.

Don't pass up the opportunity to sample some of Colorado's regional specialities while you're out and about. This includes foods like elk or deer sausage, bison burgers, Rocky Mountain oysters (bull testicles), Colorado-style green chili, and meals made with craft beer.

cuisine hygiene and safety must be taken into account while consuming street cuisine. Search for vendors that have tidy, well-kept food trucks or booths, and pay attention to how they handle their food. Additionally, be mindful of any dietary restrictions or allergies and, if required, ask about the contents.

To learn about particular street food places, timetables, and reviews, keep an eye on local event calendars, food truck groups, and internet resources. Accept Colorado's thriving street food scene and savor the variety of tastes it has to offer.

Lakes

In Colorado, there are several lakes and reservoirs where you may engage in beach-like activities and water sports. Here are a few well-known lakes in Colorado:

Cherry Creek State Park in Aurora has a sandy beach area where visitors may unwind, swim, and sunbathe. Rentals for paddleboards, kayaks, and boats are also available at the park for water activities.

The Chatfield Reservoir at Chatfield State Park (Littleton) has a permitted swimming beach with sandy coastlines and calm waves. Swimming, fishing, boating, and other water sports are available to visitors.

Horsetooth Reservoir (Fort Collins): You may swim, sunbathe, and enjoy picnics at Horsetooth Reservoir's several sandy beaches and coves. Boating, fishing, and hiking are among popular activities around the reservoir.

Boulder Reservoir (Boulder): During the summer, Boulder Reservoir has a sandy beach area with lifeguards on duty. Swimmers, paddleboarders, sailors, and beach bums are all welcome.

Carter Lake (Loveland) has a sandy swimming beach where you may relax and enjoy the water. Additionally, boating, fishing, and camping are quite popular around the lake.

Although these places provide beach-like sensations, it's vital to keep in mind that they lack ocean waves and seawater. Additionally, the seasons might affect the water temperatures in these lakes, so it's a good idea to research local laws and conditions before making travel arrangements.

The warm summer months, from late spring through early October, are when Colorado's lakes and reservoirs are usually open. It is advised to bring sunscreen, towels, beach chairs, and other necessary water sports gear. Remember to observe safety precautions, such as donning life jackets while engaging in water sports and abiding by park laws and regulations.

Colorado may not have ocean beaches, but it does have beautiful natural scenery and outdoor leisure choices. So even if there aren't any beaches along the coast, Colorado's lakes and reservoirs are still beautiful and provide a cool aquatic experience.

Luxury Travel Ideas

Here are some suggestions to make your vacation more enjoyable if you're seeking for a luxurious travel experience in Colorado:

Luxury Hotels, Resorts, Lodges, and Boutique Properties: These establishments provide top-notch facilities, first-rate service, and stunning settings. The Broadmoor in Colorado Springs, The Ritz-Carlton Bachelor Gulch in Beaver Creek, or The Little Nell in Aspen are examples of prominent hotels.

Private Transportation: To guarantee a smooth and opulent trip experience, make arrangements for private transportation services. In order to add a more opulent touch, this may also include private airport transfers, chauffeured automobile services, or even helicopter or private aircraft charters.

Fine Dining: Colorado has a thriving restaurant industry, with several luxury eateries run by renowned chefs. Enjoy delicious meals made with ingredients that are obtained locally, great wine pairings, and first-rate service. Visit upscale restaurants in places like Denver, Boulder, Aspen, and Vail.

Spa and wellness retreats: Spoil yourself with opulent spa services and wellness excursions at upscale hotels and wellness resorts. Enjoy relaxing spaces, saunas, and other wellness services while you unwind with restorative massages, facials, and body treatments.

Exclusive Outdoor Adventures: Take part in outdoor pursuits created especially for opulent guests. This can be exclusive treks with a guide, equestrian rides, heli-skiing or snowboarding outings, or fly-fishing adventures in magnificent settings.

Private Experiences & Tours: Schedule private tours of monuments and tourist destinations to explore them at your own speed. Personalized experiences may enhance your vacation, whether it's a guided tour of a national park, a visit to a winery with a personal sommelier, or a cultural tour with a local authority.

Keep up with regional events, art exhibits, and cultural performances with VIP access to events and offerings. Get VIP admission to prestigious festivals, galas, and events to fully experience Colorado's cultural scene.

Customized Itineraries: Ask a concierge service or luxury travel agency to put together an itinerary that is based on your interests and preferences. They can help you with making reservations for lodging, setting up transportation, and organizing activities depending on the degree of luxury you choose.

Colorado boasts premium shopping areas and shops where you may discover designer labels, high-end clothing, and distinctive locally produced goods. Discover upscale shopping destinations like Denver's Cherry Creek Shopping Center or Aspen's downtown district.

Private Outdoor Experiences: The natural landscapes of Colorado provide a wealth of chances for solitary outdoor adventures. Take into account excursions like exclusive guided treks to remote locations for breath-taking vistas, stunning helicopter flights, or exclusive hot air balloon rides.

Consider booking high-end lodgings and popular places well in advance when making your luxury vacation plans. To guarantee a really opulent experience, be ready to spend on upscale activities and services and to express your preferences and expectations to service providers.

Last but not least, remember to appreciate the little things, take in Colorado's natural beauty, and enjoy the comfort and tranquility that come with your upgraded vacation experience.

Travel Tips on a Budget

Here are some suggestions to help you get the most out of your vacation to Colorado without going over your travel budget if you're planning one that's on a tight budget:

Consider visiting Colorado during off-peak seasons when it's less congested. For example, shoulder seasons. You may still take in the state's beauty without the throngs that come during the busiest times of year since lodging and attractions prices are often cheaper.

Look into and contrast available accommodations: Look for inexpensive lodging options including hostels, motels, hotels, and vacation rentals. To compare costs, read reviews, and locate the finest offers that fit your budget, use online travel booking sites.

Use public transportation: Cities in Colorado with good public transit networks include Boulder and Denver. Use the buses, light rail, or free shuttles to get about without having to pay to hire a vehicle. Additionally, in cities with pedestrian-friendly neighborhoods, think about biking or walking.

Make your own food or dine at cheap restaurants: By choosing self-catering lodgings where you can cook your own meals, you may save money on food. Use your neighborhood supermarkets or farmers markets to get fresh food. When going out to dine, look for informal cafes, food trucks, or local restaurants that are reasonably priced and provide excellent value.

Take advantage of free or inexpensive attractions: Colorado offers many outdoor attractions and areas of natural beauty that don't charge high entry prices. Discover free attractions including municipal parks, public art exhibitions, or historic sites, as well as public parks, hiking trails, and beautiful overlooks.

Plan some outdoor activities; Colorado is well-known for its inexpensive or free outdoor activities. Enjoy nature hikes, riding, hiking, picnics, or just enjoying the state's breathtaking scenery.

Look for reduced or free cultural events: Consult your community's event calendar to find discounted or free cultural gatherings like concerts, festivals, and art shows. Regular open-to-the-public community events are held in many Colorado communities, providing a window into the area's culture and artistic environment.

Utilize travel specials and discounts: Be on the lookout for travel offers, cheap attraction passes, or package packages that provide discounts on lodging, travel, and entertainment. For special offers and discounts, check the websites of tourist boards, neighborhood visitor centers, or travel websites.

Pack sensibly: Include necessities like a reusable water bottle, sunscreen, a pair of good walking shoes, and layers of clothes that are suited for Colorado's constantly changing weather. This will assist you in lowering your trip-related expenditures.

Take advantage of Colorado's natural beauty by participating in free or inexpensive outdoor activities like hiking, biking, fishing, or picnicking in parks and open spaces. You don't need to buy pricey equipment since many places provide free or inexpensive equipment rentals.

Keep in mind that traveling on a budget does not imply forgoing adventures. You may explore and take advantage of Colorado's natural marvels, outdoor activities, and cultural sites without breaking the bank thanks to the state's many cheap and pleasant alternatives.

Insider advice for First timers

Here are some expert suggestions to assist first-time visitors to Colorado make the most of their visit:

Layer your clothing since Colorado's weather may be erratic, particularly in the mountains. Layer your clothing to prepare for changing temperatures. This will make it simple for you to change your outfit when the weather changes throughout the day.

Because of Colorado's high altitude, it's important to stay hydrated. Keep hydrated by carrying a reusable water bottle and drinking plenty of water, particularly while participating in outdoor activities. Limiting your consumption of alcohol and caffeine is also a good idea since these substances may worsen dehydration at higher elevations.

If you're coming from a lower height, allow yourself some time to adjust to the higher altitude. Take it easy while you're at higher altitudes. During the first day or two, go easy to give your body time to acclimate. Avoid overworking yourself and be alert for any altitude sickness symptoms, such as fainting or breathing difficulties. Keep hydrated and think about taking breaks as necessary.

Colorado is notorious for its swift weather changes, so prepare for them. Even though the day begins bright, a thunderstorm or temperature decrease might develop suddenly. Before leaving, check the weather forecast and be ready with rain gear, sunscreen, hats, and coats. Always carry a little backpack with your necessities in it.

Colorado takes pride in its natural beauty and outdoor places, so please treat them with respect. Picking up your rubbish, keeping on paths that have been established, and showing care for animals are all examples of leaving no trace. In order for future generations to appreciate Colorado's unspoiled environment, please help.

Prepare for outdoor activities by doing your research and making a plan in advance if you want to go hiking or camping. Verify the trail's conditions, bring the appropriate supplies, and be informed of any permits or rules. Additionally, it is a good idea to let someone know your plans, particularly if you plan to go to a distant location.

The food culture in Colorado is varied, so give it a try. Don't pass up the chance to sample regional delicacies like Rocky Mountain oysters, bison burgers, Colorado green chili, and artisan beers from the numerous breweries. For handcrafted goods and fresh food, check out your neighborhood farmers markets.

Don't forget to schedule time for relaxation and acclimatization. Colorado's magnificent vistas and outdoor activities might be alluring, but don't forget to schedule time for both.

Enjoy the breathtaking scenery, inhale the clean mountain air, and give yourself permission to relax in the peace of nature.

Engage the community: Coloradans are renowned for their warmth and love of the outdoors. Talk to the locals, get their advice, and find out about the area's best-kept secrets. Locals can add to your Colorado experience and provide insightful advice.

Colorado is a haven for outdoor enthusiasts, so embrace the experience. Be adventurous and open to new experiences. Push your limits and engage in sports like mountain biking, whitewater rafting, skiing, or hiking to make lifelong memories.

Consider the variety of things Colorado has to offer, from outdoor excursions to cultural pleasures. You'll be ready to make the most of your first trip to this stunning state with the help of this insider advice. Enjoy the journey!

7-day itinerary plan

An example itinerary for your trip to Colorado is provided below:

Day 1: Getting to Denver

Arrive at Colorado's state capital, Denver.
Discover downtown Denver, including the Denver Art Museum, Larimer Square, and 16th Street Mall.
Visit a neighborhood brewery or have dinner at a famous Denver restaurant.

Day 2: Rocky Mountain National Park

Drive the 1.5 hours from Denver to Rocky Mountain National Park.

Explore the park's picturesque paths, lakes, and vistas all day long.

Don't overlook well-known sights like Bear Lake, Trail Ridge Road, and the Alpine Visitor Center.

For a more immersive experience, consider trekking to places like Sky Pond or Emerald Lake.

Day 3: Manitou Springs and Colorado Springs

Drive the 1.5-hour distance from Denver to Colorado Springs.

Visit the beautiful natural rock formation park known as the Garden of the Gods.

Hike or take the cog train to the top of Pikes Peak, known as "America's Mountain."

Discover Manitou Springs, a quaint community famous for its art galleries, boutiques, and natural springs.

Day 4: Mesa Verde National Park

From Colorado Springs, travel southwest for roughly 6 hours to Mesa Verde National Park, a UNESCO World Heritage Site.

Discover the history and culture of the ancestors of the Pueblo people by touring the historic cliff homes.

If you want to learn more about the amazing ancient sites in the park, join a ranger-led tour.

Day 5: Silverton and Durango

One and a half hours' drive from Mesa Verde lies the ancient town of Durango, which is tucked away in the San Juan Mountains.

The Durango & Silverton Narrow Gauge Railroad offers beautiful mountain vistas as you go along on a picturesque train journey.

Discover Durango's quaint streets, stop by neighborhood stores, and have lunch at one of the town's eateries.

Day 6: Aspen

About 4.5 hours from Durango, you may go to Aspen, which is renowned for its natural beauty and outdoor activity.
Take a day trip to the nearby mountains to go hiking or riding.
Visit Independence Pass for a picturesque drive for breathtaking Rocky Mountain vistas.
Enjoy the lively ambiance of Aspen's downtown, which has restaurants, shops, and art galleries.

Day 7:Boulder and departure

Drive to Boulder, which is three hours' drive from Aspen.
Discover the pedestrian-only Pearl Street Mall, which is populated with stores, eateries, and street performers.
Enjoy the energetic college town environment by visiting the University of Colorado Boulder campus.

Leave from the Denver International Airport, or if you choose, stay longer in Boulder.

Please keep in mind that this schedule is only a recommendation that may be changed in accordance with your choices, time limits, and particular interests. Prior to your visit, it's a good idea to confirm the operating times, the state of the roads, and any special prerequisites for any attractions or activities.

Dos and Don'ts

Following are some suggestions for doing and not doing when visiting Colorado:

Dos:

Do remain hydrated and drink plenty of water, particularly at higher elevations.

Do layer your clothing to account for the varying weather conditions.

Do observe the principles of Leave No Trace and respect the environment.

Do look at the weather predictions, and be ready for abrupt weather changes.

Engage the community and get advice from residents to improve your experience.

Try the regional food and drink, particularly the Colorado delicacies and artisan brews.

Do your study on the hiking routes, activities, and sights before your trip.

Do protect yourself from sunburn by using sunscreen, hats, and sunglasses.

In national parks and other protected places, you must abide by all laws and regulations.

Do take advantage of Colorado's scenic landscape and outdoor activities.

Don'ts:

Overlooking the consequences of high altitude is dangerous. Be mindful of the signs of altitude sickness and give yourself time to adapt.

Avoid littering and leaving garbage behind. Respect the environment and dispose of rubbish correctly.

Never approach or feed animals. Keep a safe distance and watch animals from afar.
Check to see whether any specific activities or attractions need reservations or permits.

Don't undervalue the significance of travel insurance, particularly if you plan to engage in outdoor sports like skiing or hiking.

Never enter forbidden places or infringe on private property.
Never undervalue the power of the natural world. Follow safety precautions while engaging in outdoor activities.

In rural places, don't depend only on GPS guidance. Be prepared for spotty mobile coverage and carry maps.

Don't disregard your physical health. Some outdoor activities call for a particular amount of preparation and fitness.

Remember to respect regional traditions and cultural sensitivity.
You may have a safe, fun, and polite experience when visiting Colorado if you bear these dos and don'ts in mind.

Currency

The US Dollar (USD) is the unit of money used in Colorado and the whole United States. In hotels, restaurants, stores, and other venues, it is frequently accepted. Most establishments readily take credit cards including Visa, MasterCard, American Express, and Discover. You may withdraw money in USD through ATMs, which are extensively distributed in cities and towns. To prevent any problems with card transactions, it is important to let your bank or credit card provider know about your vacation intentions. Furthermore, it's a good idea to have some small-denomination cash on hand for smaller businesses or locations that may not take credit cards.

Tipping and telephone use

Tipping: In Colorado and around the country, tipping is traditional. Following are some suggestions for tipping:

In restaurants, depending on the level of service, tips often range from 15% to 20% of the final bill before taxes. Be cautious to check the bill since some eateries may add a tip fee for bigger parties.

In bars, it's customary to give the bartender $1 to $2 each drink, or around 15% to 20% of the overall amount if you're running a tab.

Hotels: It's traditional to give the bellhop or porter who helps with baggage a gratuity, often between $1 and $2 per bag. $2 to $5 each day of your stay may be placed in an envelope with a letter for the housekeeping crew.

Transportation: The standard gratuity for cab and ridesharing drivers is between 15% and 20% of the fare. A $2–$5 gratuity is typical for such services like valet parking and airport transfers.

Other Services: Tipping is also typical for personal services like getting your hair done, getting a spa treatment, hiring a tour guide, etc. Although tips might vary, it's customary to leave between 15% and 20%.

Remember that leaving a tip is a way to express gratitude for excellent treatment, so feel free to modify the amount according to the level of service you get.

Telecommunications: In Colorado, you may choose from a wide range of mobile phone service provider alternatives and dependable coverage. In the majority of urban and suburban locations, major carriers like AT&T, Verizon, T-Mobile, and Sprint provide strong coverage.

If you are going abroad, it is crucial to inquire about international roaming options with your cell service provider or to think about getting a local SIM card for cheaper costs.

The majority of hotels, eateries, cafés, and public areas in Colorado provide internet connection in addition to mobile phone services. There is free Wi-Fi accessible in many places, and there are also paid Wi-Fi alternatives in other places.

Internet-based calling services like WhatsApp, Skype, or FaceTime may be more affordable than conventional phone calls if you need to make international calls. If you are not using

Wi-Fi, be wary of any data consumption fees.

To make sure you have the essential connection throughout your stay in Colorado, it is advised that you contact your cell service provider in advance to inquire about international plans, roaming fees, and any other special information.

Dress code and photography advice

Photographic Advice:

Capture the Scenic Beauty: Colorado is home to beautiful natural scenery. If you want to capture the immensity of the mountains, canyons, and other beautiful views, make sure to pack a camera with a wide-angle lens.

Timing Is Crucial Planning your photographs should take the lighting conditions into account. Long shadows and soft, warm light are best captured in the early morning and late afternoon. Furthermore, dawn and sunset may provide striking sky hues.

Investigate Diverse Points of View: Don't be scared to try out various perspectives and viewpoints. To take pictures that are special and fascinating, go down low, climb up high, or explore various viewpoint points.

Wildlife photography: Elk, moose, deer, bighorn sheep, and many bird species may all be found in Colorado. If you're interested in photographing wildlife, practice patience, keep your distance, and respect the animals' environment and natural habits.

Capture the Seasons: Each of Colorado's four different seasons has its own unique charm. Make careful to capture the variety of the seasons, including the bright autumn foliage, the snowy winter vistas, and the vibrant spring blossoms.

Dresscode:
Colorado's dress code is typically informal and laidback, however it may change based on the setting and the event. Following are some general principles:

Outdoor Activities: It's crucial to dress correctly if you want to go hiking, riding, or engage in other outdoor activities. Wear durable shoes or hiking boots, comfortable, moisture-wicking gear, and think about layering so you can adjust to changing weather conditions.

Urban Areas: The dress code is often informal and relaxed in places like Denver, Boulder, and Colorado Springs. It's typical to wear jeans, t-shirts, and casual footwear. However, somewhat dressier apparel, such as smart casual or business casual, may be suitable for more formal events or upmarket restaurants.

Mountain resorts: The dress code might be a little more upmarket and fashionable while visiting mountain resort cities like Aspen or Vail. People wear ski gear and après-ski clothes throughout the winter skiing season. Resort casual attire is typical throughout the summer.

Cultural Events or Fine Dining: It is advisable to dress a little more formally for cultural events, museums, or fine dining venues. Women may choose from dresses, skirts, or fancy pants, while males can wear slacks or khakis with a collared shirt.

Colorado is known for its laid-back and active lifestyle, so most occasions call for casual, functional attire. However, it's a good idea to always double-check the precise attire requirements for any special events or activities you want to participate in while you're there.

Useful words

The following words and phrases may be helpful when you are visiting Colorado for non English speaking Individuals:

Hello! - "Hello!"
Thank you - "Thank you."
Please - "Please."
Excuse me - "Excuse me."
Do you speak English? - "Do you speak English?"
Where is the restroom? - "Where is the restroom?"
How much does it cost? - "How much does it cost?"
Can you help me? - "Can you help me?"
I'm sorry - "I'm sorry."

I don't understand - "I don't understand."

What's your recommendation? - "What's your recommendation?"

Can I have the check, please? - "Can I have the check, please?"

Where is the nearest ATM? - "Where is the nearest ATM?"

Could you repeat that, please? - "Could you repeat that, please?"

I need a taxi - "I need a taxi."

Is there Wi-Fi here? - "Is there Wi-Fi here?"

Can I have a menu, please? - "Can I have a menu, please?"

Is it possible to pay by credit card? - "Is it possible to pay by credit card?"

What time does it open/close? - "What time does it open/close?"

Have a nice day! - "Have a nice day!"

Using these words should make it easier for you to engage with people in Colorado and communicate successfully.

Emergency services

Here are the crucial emergency contact numbers in Colorado in case of an emergency:

Call 911 for emergency services (police, fire, and medical).
In the event of any emergency requiring urgent police, fire, or medical help, phone this number.

Non-Emergency Police Assistance: Depending on the city or county you are in, you may call a different non-emergency number for the local police department. It's a good idea to find and note the non-emergency phone number for the region you're visiting.

Call the Poison Control Center at 1-800-222-1222.

By dialing this number, you may contact the poison control center, which offers quick help and direction in the event of poisoning or the consumption of harmful chemicals.

Roadside help: If your automobile breaks down or you need roadside help, call your auto insurance company or an organization like AAA (American Automobile Association).

Medical Emergencies: You may also get in touch with the local hospital or healthcare institution that is closest to you if you need medical help. It is a good idea to preserve or have handy the phone numbers for any local hospitals or clinics.

Remember that calling 911 is the most important thing to do in an emergency. The emergency services operator will help you through the problem and send the right assistance your way.

Facts about Colorado

Here are some intriguing Colorado-related facts:

Colorado is known as the "Centennial State" because it joined the Union as the 38th state on August 1, 1876, precisely 100 years after the Declaration of Independence was ratified.

Rocky Mountain High: With more than 50 peaks rising to an altitude of 14,000 feet or more, Colorado is renowned for its magnificent Rocky Mountains. These "Fourteeners," as they are sometimes referred as, provide great hiking and climbing chances.

Denver is the biggest city and the state capital of Colorado. Its elevation, which is around one mile above sea level, gives it the moniker "Mile High City."

Colorado is divided into two drainage basins by the Continental Divide, which runs across the state. East side water goes to the Atlantic Ocean, while west side water travels to the Pacific Ocean.

Rocky Mountain National Park, Mesa Verde National Park, Great Sand Dunes National Park and Preserve, and Black Canyon of the Gunnison National Park are the four national parks that may be found in Colorado. The different landscapes and natural treasures of the state are shown in these parks.

Craft Beer Mecca: Colorado is home to more than 400 breweries and a robust craft beer scene. The biggest beer festival and competition in the nation is the Great American Beer Festival, which takes place yearly in Denver.

Outdoor Recreation: Colorado provides a variety of outdoor recreational pursuits, such as rock climbing, fishing, mountain biking, skiing, and snowboarding. The state is a sanctuary for outdoor enthusiasts because to its wealth of natural beauty and diverse topography.

Marijuana legalization: Colorado was one of the first states in the US to legalize marijuana for recreational use in 2012. As a result, the state's cannabis tourist sector is expanding.

Dinosaur Fossils: Colorado is home to a number of paleontological sites and a wealth of dinosaur fossils, including the Florissant Fossil Beds National Monument and Dinosaur National Monument. These locations provide insightful perspectives into the ancient world.

Olympic Heritage: Colorado has a long history with winter sports and has previously played home to the Winter Olympics. Denver was initially chosen to host the 1976 Winter Olympics but eventually turned it down because of budgetary issues.

These facts only touch on a small portion of Colorado's extensive history, stunning scenery, fun activities, and cultural relevance.

Conclusion

In conclusion, Colorado provides tourists with a unique and alluring vacation experience. The state is brimming with natural marvels, outdoor experiences, cultural attractions, and a warm and friendly environment, from its breathtaking Rocky Mountains to its dynamic cities and quaint communities. Colorado has something to offer everyone, whether they are looking for exhilarating outdoor pursuits like hiking, skiing, or rafting, iconic landmarks like Mesa Verde or Rocky Mountain National Park, indulging in the state's craft beer and culinary scene, or getting lost in its art, music, and festivals. Travelers of all interests and ages will find the state to be a perfect visit because of its distinctive terrain, rich history, and welcoming people. So gather your belongings, embrace the spirit of exploration, and get ready to make priceless memories in the stunning state of Colorado.